DEEP STATE
TARGET

DEEP STATE
TARGET

How I Got Caught in the Crosshairs of the
Plot to Bring Down President Trump

GEORGE PAPADOPOULOS

DIVERSION
BOOKS

Diversion Books
A Division of Diversion Publishing Corp.
443 Park Avenue South, Suite 1004
New York, New York 10016
www.DiversionBooks.com

For more information, email info@diversionbooks.com

Book design by Pauline Neuwirth, Neuwirth & Associates.

First Diversion Books edition March 2019.
Hardcover ISBN: 978-1-63576-493-2
eBook ISBN: 978-1-63576-494-9

Printed in the U.S.A.
1 3 5 7 9 10 8 6 4 2

To my wife, Simona,
who has been my rock through this entire saga

CONTENTS

DEEP STATE
TARGET

PROLOGUE

"IT'S NOT SO bad here."

My cellmate's a skinny guy with a thing for tattoos. He also has a thing for narcotics, apparently, because he's already told me he's facing seven years for drug possession.

"The chicken wings they serve on Wednesdays are really good," he reassures me.

Our other cellmates—a guy who can't stop talking about the Bible, a Hispanic guy who doesn't speak much English, and a rambling maniac who claims to have worked for the State Department—all nod in agreement.

"Spicy but not too spicy."

"They are the shit!"

"Amen!"

I don't give a damn about the chicken wings. When you find yourself shell-shocked and sleep deprived in a holding cell and told you're facing twenty-five years in prison, you have other things on your mind besides food.

On the other hand, this chicken wing soliloquy is about the only thing that has made any sense in the last twenty-four hours.

One day earlier, on July 27, 2017, I had flown into Dulles Airport, ending the second leg of my Athens to Munich to D.C. to Chicago flight plan. When I disembarked, a team of FBI hustled me off to a secluded area of the airport and immediately tore through my briefcase and bags, feverishly searching for something. I watched the agents rifle through my bags twice. Then I watched them confer with each other, agitated looks on their faces. It was clear to me that they'd expected to find something important. It was equally clear from their pissed-off expressions that they hadn't found it.

My mind was reeling. What the hell were they looking for? Just days earlier, cutting short a vacation with the love of my life on the island of Mykonos, I had gone to Israel to meet a man who said he wanted to do business. He summoned me to his hotel room in Tel Aviv and gave me $10,000 as a retainer. In cash. Unsure of his motives or associations, I had left the money with a lawyer in Greece and headed home. Was that what the FBI expected to find? A load of undeclared cash? And if so, how did they know to look for it? Was it all some kind of setup?

They handcuffed me and shackled my ankles. I spotted the two agents who had interviewed me months earlier in Chicago. When I asked them what was going on, I got no answer. When I repeated my question, another agent sneered, "This is what happens when you work for Trump."

Again, my mind was flying in a dozen directions. As a member of Donald Trump's foreign policy advisory team, I had helped set up meetings with foreign heads of state. I had defended the candidate against governments that had criticized him. I had met with foreign ministers and senior diplomats and had attended international conferences and embassy parties. I couldn't think of anything I'd done that had broken the law. Hell, I don't even smoke pot.

I asked again: What had I done, and why was I being arrested? "This is what happens when you work with Russians," a G-man taunted me.

That answer sent me into a further panic. Russians? The agents in Chicago had asked me about Russians. And they'd asked what I'd heard about Russians. And then—over and over and over—they had asked who I had talked to about what I had heard.

As I remembered it, I had told investigators that in the last year, while working as a foreign policy advisor for the campaign, I had met a number of people who claimed to have connections to the Russian government. But as far as I knew, I had met only one Russian in my entire life—although when I think back on it, I'm not even certain she really was Russian.

Until that moment in Dulles Airport—an army of men in black basically accusing me of working with Russians—I don't think I knew what real terror was. I was about to get a crash course.

Terror is facing the complete unknown and having all your assumptions turned upside down.

It's the FBI telling you that you are under arrest without telling you what you've done.

It's being hauled off in a black SUV.

It's asking to be able to contact your girlfriend and your family and realizing nobody is going to lift a finger for you.

It's suddenly wondering if the people you thought you were working with to further the agenda of a presidential candidate—to create positive relationships to further American interests—are not who they pretended to be.

It's going before a judge and waiting—because the famous dream-team prosecutors working for Robert Mueller are more than an hour late filing charges, evidently struggling to figure out what charges to file.

It's hearing prosecutors say you are going to face twenty-five years in prison.

It's being charged with lying to FBI investigators and having no idea what you lied about.

It's having no one believe you—even when you are telling the absolute truth.

It's realizing you've had a target on your back for more than a year—but having no idea why it's there or who is aiming at you.

In other words, terror is when absolutely nothing makes any sense and you lose faith that it ever will.

So, about those chicken wings: I laugh about it now—the idea that all I might have had to look forward to in life were Wednesday's chicken wings while I served out a long prison sentence. But my fellow inmates, bless them one and all, were truly human. They were talking about comfort food and trying to help a totally freaked-out newcomer look on the bright side.

Even when none seemed to exist.

Compared to the aggressive, threatening, uncommunicative lawmen who tossed me in a prison cell without telling me why, the gourmands of that Iron Bar Hotel weren't criminals, they were cellblock buddies.

At least they made sense.

It's taken me a long time to figure out what led to my arrest. I realize that I misspoke to the FBI, but I wasn't lying to hide anything other than an extremely irritating and embarrassing cat-and-mouse game. I'll go into that in more detail, but for now, let me just say that I talked dismissively about someone who I discovered to be a charlatan. And guess what? I was right about him. But I was wrong to not fully, accurately characterize my waste-of-time interactions with this guy named Joseph Mifsud. And the "lie" I was charged with, as you'll see, certainly wasn't intentional.

But why was I a target at all? That is what has taken time to unravel—to fully understand why there was a bullseye on my back. This book explains why I was set up and who I believe was pulling the strings.

When it all started, back in 2016, I was a young, earnest, hard-working man from Chicago with a strong interest in international politics. I landed in a coveted position and suddenly found myself in a world filled with influence peddlers who seem to have stepped out of the pages of *The Maltese Falcon* and Jason Bourne novels. Almost everyone I met—and I found this out much later—had ties to intelligence outfits. Diplomats and academics recorded conversations with me. Businessmen offered me tens of thousands of dollars to work with them—without ever specifying what the work was. In the middle of all this, I met a stunning Italian woman—a brainy blonde who spoke five languages—and I became completely smitten. What happened next…well, you know a bit about the FBI. But I've left out the CIA, MI6, Australian intelligence, Turkish operatives, private intelligence companies, and a university that specializes in training spooks.

I've been portrayed in the media, often by journalists who have never met me, as naive, self-deluded, ambitious, and a self-promoter. There is, I admit, an element of truth in all of that. I was not a veteran diplomat when I began working for the Trump campaign. But I had written important policy papers and made significant connections in the diplomatic community.

I also had faith in myself. Unfortunately, I made the mistake of placing too much faith in some of the people I came in contact with, and I've paid the price for being open and unguarded.

I am ambitious—I want to excel in my work and have an impact on the world. That helped put me in a position of influence, for better and for worse. And in my line of work—consulting and facilitating collaborative energy partnerships—a little self-promotion is a necessity.

So yes: Guilty as charged. But I'm also guilty of having had some great successes both with the Trump campaign and at the Hudson Institute, a prominent Washington, D.C. think tank. That success made me a target.

Given all the mysterious encounters I've experienced in the last two-plus years—all the shady figures arranging clandestine hotel meetings, flying me here and there professing the best of intentions, dropping hundreds of dollars a night on dinners and cigars, breaking out of friendly conversations to suddenly interrogate me about "the Russians," promising to introduce me to power brokers and then going silent—I now think of myself a little differently.

I was the right guy to become the wrong man. A guy set up to become the patsy in an international espionage conspiracy.

This is my story, my nightmare, and, I hope, my redemption.

CHAPTER 1

A BEGINNING

I REMEMBER WATCHING a 2000 presidential election debate between George W. Bush and Al Gore when I was in eighth grade. I was not a middle-school policy wonk—far from it. I really didn't know much beyond what I'd learned about politics in my social studies classes and at home listening to my dad. But I remember two things about the debate: I really was impressed by Gore at first. He was articulate and came across as a very educated person. Yet despite that, there was something in George Bush's manner that made me gravitate toward him. I liked him more. He seemed much more pleasant than Gore, like he was the warmer guy who would connect well with Americans. I mention this mini-awakening because I think it may resonate with others who are moved by a personality, not a policy. Years later, I would react positively to another candidate with a unique persona.

Although I graduated from Niles West High School in Skokie, Illinois, I was in ninth grade at Hinsdale Central High School when—sitting in biology class—I heard about the 9/11 attack. I was horrified and enraged. For the first time in my life, I was aware that I felt a sense of national pride. I was fourteen years old, amped by outrage, injustice, and the carnage. I started to understand what it means to be an American. To recognize the privilege of living in a country where we have freedom of speech, where my own immigrant family was able to settle, safely, securely, and attain a remarkable amount of affluence. We were "united" by this country and these laws. I couldn't believe foreigners were attacking our country—a land like no other, with guaranteed freedoms of religion and the press and the right to live in the pursuit of happiness. I felt proud to be part of this country. I wanted to support it, this place, my homeland.

I know I wasn't alone in my reaction. As everyone remembers, there was an enormously powerful, national, rally-round-the-flag response. Everywhere, with everyone. But as a young teenager, I felt it profoundly—like falling in love for the first time. And also, for the first time, I thought that maybe life had something else in store for me instead of becoming a doctor. This was heresy in my immediate family, where practicing medicine was seen as my destiny—following in the footsteps of my grandfather, my father, and, later, my brother. But it was the beginning of an awakening. I had begun to realize that I didn't want to follow the family medical school path. My father's first cousin, Vasilis Papadopoulos, worked for many years at the European Commission, and so did other relatives. Meanwhile, my uncle Alex Papadopoulos had a PhD from the University of Chicago in geography, and he frequently taught classes that touched on wealth, power, and the world.

Maybe I wanted to get into the other "family business"—politics.

LONDON SWINGS

When I graduated from DePaul University with a degree in political science, I had my sights set on diplomacy and politics. So I enrolled at the University College London's School of Public Policy. It didn't take me long to realize I was more interested in security and geopolitical issues, so I switched to the school's security studies program.

I loved the courses, my classmates, and the city itself. London felt like the most cosmopolitan, international city on the planet to me. I was a twenty-two-year-old kid from the suburbs of Chicago, and now I was having discussions with people from all over the world, many of whom had direct connections to the corridors of power. One of my classmates was the son of the Sri Lankan minister of defense. Another was the son of the mayor of Tbilisi, the capital of the Republic of Georgia. There were a bunch of Israelis, fresh out of the military. The closest I had ever been to any political power before this was when my father hosted a fundraiser in our home for the now-disgraced congressman Dennis Hastert, who was the Speaker of the House at the time. Now I was making my own real connections to people who inhabited the worlds of politics, diplomacy, and power. It was a heady experience for me, and I wanted more of this life.

I returned to Chicago to write my master of science thesis on the rise and fall of Islamist governments in the wake of the Arab Spring. I relished the research into a model of governance that stripped citizens of civil rights and had little in common with America's fundamental values. The paper, which was well received, would come in handy on a professional level when I later advised governments on the fall of Egyptian president Morsi and the rise of Field Marshal Sisi.

I began to think, reluctantly, about the inevitable next step: law school. Although it seems like a natural progression for someone interested in politics to understand the laws that govern our nation, I wasn't sure I wanted to spend the next three years studying the law. I wanted to be more engaged with the world and with work. Right then.

I wrote letters to dozens and dozens of think tanks and research institutes. It was 2010, and the economy was still hobbling after the 2008 fiscal meltdown. With my job search faltering, I began taking LSAT practice tests.

I was sitting in a bookstore grabbing coffee when an older man about sixty years old spotted my LSAT practice guide on the table.

"Law school? Don't go to law school," he said, taking a seat at the next table. "I'm a lawyer. It's not worth it. Maybe for some people it is, but not for me. You work long hours. You overcharge clients because you can. And the government bureaucracy exists to bill more hours! Sometimes I think it's a kickback scheme. Trials are delayed, postponed, reordered, and who pays? First the client. Then the law firm pays the government in taxes—that's the kickback!"

He was a bit of a crank. But he also struck me as completely sincere. He said that law school might actually be the worst part of the whole process because the pressure of the experience strips the joy from being young.

"I should have been traveling. Seeing the world! There are so many more interesting topics and things to do in the world than being stuck in law school and then working like a pig. Instead, I was running up a lot of debt. And if you don't land with a big firm, that debt can hang around. It did for me. So watch yourself."

I had no idea who this gentleman was. But he seemed intent on giving me friendly advice. It was, to be honest, a perspective I'd never heard. The well-dressed lawyers on TV never seem to have regrets about their position. Other than Jimmy McGill in *Better Call Saul*, that is.

As luck would have it, later that very same day I received an email from a man named Richard Weitz at the Hudson Institute think tank and research center. He liked my résumé and asked if I would be interested in working remotely, helping him research a number of foreign policy papers he was working on as the Institute's Director of the Center for Political-Military Analysis. We talked on the phone soon thereafter, and the conversation went very well.

I couldn't help thinking about the words of that mysterious lawyer from earlier in the day. This seemed like a sign. A potential reprieve, even, from law school. I would only be, technically, an intern for the institute, but I didn't care. It was a start. It put me a step closer to Washington and the kind of work I envisioned myself doing.

And it's where the story of my ascent into the world of foreign policy, presidential campaigns, and partisan politics—and the chilling spy games that unfold in the shadows—begins.

CHAPTER 2

MR. PAPADOPOULOS GOES TO WASHINGTON

I T'S THE SUMMER of 2011. And after months of collaboration and working on articles relating to nuclear nonproliferation, NATO, and China relations with Taiwan now on my résumé, Weitz invites me to attend a conference in D.C. I visit him at the institute with a goal in mind. I need paying work.

The Hudson Institute was founded in 1961 in the New York suburb of Croton-on-Hudson by nuclear strategist and futurist Herman Kahn. A former analyst for the RAND Corporation, Kahn leaped into prominence for his controversial book *On Thermonuclear War,* which, among other things, envisioned a Doomsday Machine and examined how America should plan for such a catastrophic event. The institute relocated to D.C. in 2004 and established itself as one of the leading conservative American think tanks, focusing on national security, leadership, and global engagement.

During my visit, Weitz introduces me to a man named Seth Cropsey, who had served as deputy undersecretary of the US Navy in the Reagan and Bush administrations and had worked as a fellow for the Heritage Foundation. He is in his sixties, but despite our age gap, we hit it off. We're both from Chicago, and his father, Joseph Cropsey, was a political theorist at the University of Chicago where my uncle got his geography PhD. As it happens, Seth not only helps me with my writing and thinking, he ultimately changes the direction of my life. He is working on a book at the time, *Mayday*, about the decline of US naval supremacy, and asks if I'll help him with research.

Seth also explains the inner workings of the Hudson Institute and how fellows are funded. The institute is in many ways a nonprofit consulting firm. Donors fund the research, and bringing in clients is essential to obtaining the kind of research analyst position that I was suited for. Essentially, I need to fundraise to create a position for myself—to find my own sponsors. That is a bit of a blow. The good news, though, is that I leave with the sense that Seth and others at the institute think I might be a good fit.

But how does a kid from Chicago crack into D.C.'s clubby, policy-shaping world, where everyone seems to be an ex-Pentagon official, law school graduate, or have connections to a previous presidential administration or congressman? And who can I induce to hire me to create position papers? First, I need an angle, an agenda, an insight to make people stand up and take notice.

A NEW VISION

I start to think critically about American foreign policy and my vision of the world. I am drawn to Greece and the Mediterranean theater.

My name, obviously, broadcasts my family's Greek roots, which run deep on both sides of my family. My father's grandparents left their hometown of Thessaloniki, in northern Greece, during World War II and settled in the Belgian Congo, where they ran a number of successful businesses.

My grandmother's parents—yes, they were named Anthony and Cleopatra—eventually divested in their various enterprises and moved back to Greece. My grandmother married my grandfather and went to France where he trained as a surgeon. That is where my dad, Antonios, was born. Eventually they moved back to Thessaloniki, but at age eighteen, he moved to Brussels to begin his medical studies.

My mother, Kate, was born in Greece. Her parents, Konstantinos and Demetra Bouroukas, were more blue collar. They immigrated to the United States with the clothes on their back and three young children in tow. Like so many other immigrants that built our nation, they were determined to turn the American Dream into a reality. My grandfather got a job as a painter. Eventually, he became a painting contractor. He saved money and bought property in Chicago, gradually developing a small real estate empire. He and my grandmother became self-made millionaires. My mother, Kate, continues working in real estate to this day.

My parents met in Boston. My father was completing his medical residency at Tufts University, and my mother was in town visiting relatives when they met at a dance. They married and settled in Chicago, where I was born in 1987. We didn't stay in town long; my father, a Greek citizen, had to complete his compulsory military service, so we relocated to Thessaloniki for two years. We moved back to Chicago just before I entered kindergarten. At the time, my Greek was better than my English.

America, for years, has given short-shrift to Greece and aligned itself with Turkey and Israel. Those two countries shared a quiet, under-the-radar coexistence for decades. But in 2010, the hidden ties between the two nations started to fray. Israelis were found to be aiding Kurds—long a political problem for Turkey—in Iraq, along the Turkish border. Meanwhile, pro-Palestinian activists, including the Turkish Foundation for Human Rights and Freedoms and Humanitarian Relief, launched a flotilla of six ships intended to deliver aid to the Gaza Strip, defying a blockade instituted by Israel and Egypt.

The Israeli Navy's Flotilla 13 unit stormed one of the Turkish ships, the *Mavi Marmara,* and all hell broke loose. Ten activists died. A number of Israeli commandos were injured. The flotilla and the raid generated international headlines, and relations between Israel and Turkey hit a new low.

Also in 2010, Noble Energy, a Texas-based company, announced that the recently discovered natural gas fields off the coast of the tiny nation's Mediterranean coastline, later named "Leviathan" and "Tamar," far exceeded earlier expectations. This discovery set off enormous shock waves in the energy business. It meant total energy independence for Israel and a new source of natural gas for the international market.

Meanwhile, in Turkey, Recep Tayyip Erdoğan, Turkey's prime minister since 2004, was consolidating power. Turkey has been held to the West as the ideal model for secular Muslim democracy. But that vision has become blurred. Erdoğan is an Islamist. He believes in Islamic law. For another, he has anti-democratic, strongman tendencies. His record for quashing opposition is well-documented.

Despite these realities, President Obama's administration continued working with Turkey.

It is hard not to see Erdoğan in the same light as so many other Muslim leaders who embrace Islamic law. Sadly, very few of these countries have proven to be friendly to democracy or American interests. Look at Pakistan, Libya, and Iran. Saudi Arabia, for all the money it spends in the West, isn't any better; it may be the most anti-Western, repressive country on the planet. As much as I was gung-ho about the invasion of Iraq, it is now quite clear that the Iraqi War, tragically, was a huge mistake. Bush may have had the best intentions, but his war destabilized the Middle East, cost America billions of dollars and thousands of lives, and failed to bring true democracy to a region that—judging from all recent fallout—has scant interest in civil liberties and freedom.

Given all this, when I look at a map of the Mediterranean, I wonder why Israel, Egypt, Greece, and Cyprus aren't viewed as a natural alliance? And why doesn't America seek to strengthen relations between them? Turkey, of course, has been seen as strategically vital because it controls the Bosporus Strait, which is where the Russian Navy would, theoretically, enter the Mediterranean via the Black Sea. But establishing a military presence with Greece and Cyprus would provide a substantial buffer for any Turkish delusions of grandeur in the area. As for funneling the natural gas from Israel to Turkey? Why give Turkey more strategic power?

I conclude that backing Turkey, despite its NATO membership, is not ideal for American or Israeli interests. I share my thoughts with Seth Cropsey, Richard Weitz, and Douglas Feith, the director of national security strategies at the institute. They tell me I may be onto something.

It turns out I am.

THE GREEK CONNECTION

I move to Washington at the end of 2012. I attend a Capitol Hill reception hosted by Gus Bilirakis, a Republican congressman from Florida. I am looking for contacts. Networking. You do it in business, you do it in politics; I want to be in the business of politics, so I go, thinking maybe I can find some traction within the Greek-American community.

At the reception I meet a man named Aristide Caratzas, a sharp New York-bred businessman tied to the American neoconservative movement. I ask him about his background, and he tells me he went to New York's prestigious Bronx Science High School, that he is a consultant and advisor to many business projects around the globe, and he has strong ties with Greek shipping companies. He also tells me he was friends with Michael Ledeen, an influential American Enterprise Institute neoconservative who had consulting gigs with the Pentagon and the State Department. I am impressed. Here is a Greek-American who seems connected to politicians without being tied to the Greek Orthodox Church. Now, I have nothing against the Orthodox Church, but I want to mainstream Greek influence. I want Greece to be part of the conversation because of its geopolitical and strategic importance, not because of the church. I want to turn Greek relations into a mainstream issue.

Ari asks me what I am interested in doing, and I mention that I'm interested in the offshore gas found in Israel and Cyprus, the collapse of Israeli-Turkish relations, and how this seems like a great moment to promote an initiative between Greece, Cyprus, and Israel. I suggest that there's an opportunity for the United States to support those countries and vice versa.

Ari likes these ideas. He says, "Let me see what I can do, and I'll get back to you."

We exchange business cards. I remember thinking, "Wow, that would be amazing." But I also remember thinking, what are the odds?

A week or so later, Ari visits the institute and meets with John Walters, the vice president of the Hudson Institute.

"I'll put up $100,000 for this project," Ari says. "And on your end, the project is going to be a monograph about supporting this new relationship between Greece, Cyprus, Israel, and pitching Greece as the new frontier for the sixth fleet in the Mediterranean—not Italy and Turkey. Then you're going to host a conference, brief everyone on Capitol Hill."

When the meeting ends, I get a literal pat on the back from John Walters. Seth is smiling. I'm about to turn twenty-five, and I've just come up with $100,000 of work for the institute. I have my first job. I'm officially a research associate at the Hudson Institute. "Run with it; it's your project," Walters tells me.

These are the words I want to hear. I am determined to hustle and make things happen. I want to prove myself and deliver something for Ari, the first guy to truly believe in me and my ideas. I have a dream now. A plan. My goal is to influence the most powerful conservatives in the country, to realign the thought process of politicians and analysts who've adored Turkey for so long and convince them that Erdoğan's Islamist anti-democratic stance is terrible for us and bad for Israel.

It is a challenge because it means policy experts are going to have to flip. One of them is the institute's own Douglas Feith, who was former undersecretary for defense policy under Donald Rumsfeld and Paul Wolfowitz. I respect these men for their service and their noble goals for the world. Sadly, they were wrong about the effects of the Iraq War. They over-estimated the appeal of democracy in the Middle East and failed to see the power and appeal of Islamist leaders in that area of the world, many of whom shrewdly provided food and shelter to their communities at a time when those in power did not. Now, years later, these influential thinkers still believe our relationship with Turkey is vital at all costs—even if it means backing a strongman who believes in Sharia law.

Still, Feith's support of our proposal would be a significant boost for us. As I expected, he is very hesitant to support our initiative. But I tell him that representatives from the Israeli embassy—including economic attaché Eli Groner, who will later become the top aid to Israeli Prime Minister Benjamin Netanyahu—have committed to attending our conference along with delegations from Greece and Cyprus. It would be the first time in history that these three countries have met to discuss an alliance—at least publicly. At the mention of Israel, Feith perks up—as if the idea instantly has become more credible. He agrees to attend the conference.

I am flying high. Things are happening. Seth and I set to work on a major fifty-two-page monograph: *U.S. Policy and the Strategic Relationship of Greece, Cyprus, and Israel: Power Shifts in the Eastern Mediterranean.*

On October 22, 2013, the conference, "Power Shifts in the Eastern Mediterranean," kicks off. The centerpiece of the event is three panels, "Political and Security Changes in the Eastern Mediterranean"; "Implications of the Emerging Strategic Relationship of Israel, Greece, and Cyprus, and Turkey's Drift Towards Authoritarianism and Islamism"; and "The Changing Eastern Mediterranean Energy Security Environment." I had arranged for both the Greek and Cypriot ambassadors to the United States—Christos Panagopoulos and George Chacalli—to attend, as well as Eli Groner from the

Israeli embassy. Also speaking on the panels are Rep. Brad Schneider, an Illinois Democrat who served on the House Foreign Affairs Committee (D-IL), Doug Feith, and other Hudson Institute heavyweights.

The event exceeds Ari's expectations, not to mention my own. To hear these influential men discussing ideas and topics that I helped shape is tremendously gratifying. I feel, in that moment, that I'm helping formulate policy and facilitate alliances. Not only that, I am correcting a misguided US policy that I believe threatens the security of the Western world.

In parallel to the conference, Seth Cropsey and I begin work on *U.S. Policy and the Strategic Relationship of Greece, Cyprus, and Israel,* which is eventually published in 2015. It crystallizes our research into this complex region and advocates a pipeline that critics dismissed as a "pipe dream." By 2018, our ideas have become a reality; instead of the pipeline going from Israel to Turkey (via Cyprus), plans are underway to build connections to Egypt and Greece.

OBAMA, EGYPT & CHAOS

There is another reason to pursue this alliance. The shake-out from the Arab Spring, which began in Tunisia in late 2010 and spilled over to Egypt in 2011, had complicated the Eastern Mediterranean. When Mohamed Morsi, the candidate of the Muslim Brotherhood, was elected president of Egypt in June 2012, the most populous Muslim nation in the region was poised to be governed by the same Islamist group that shaped Al-Qaeda leaders Osama bin Laden and his Egyptian second-in-command, Ayman al-Zawahiri. Obviously, Israel was unhappy with that development. Erdoğan, on the other hand, was thrilled. He began to finance and arm Egypt, believing he had found his cohort in Morsi and envisioning a Muslim Brotherhood alliance that Turkey would lead. Egypt was in political, social, and economic tatters at the time. Turkey saw a vacuum emerge and wanted to fill it. For some reason, Obama seemed to cling to the idea that democracy had prevailed in Egypt and that somehow Egypt, Turkey, and Israel would all sing "Kumbaya" together—which was never going to happen. So he did not appreciate any attempt to isolate Turkey.

When Morsi was overthrown by Field Marshal Abdel Fattah el-Sisi—who hated the Muslim Brotherhood—in what was essentially a military coup on July 3, 2013, relations with Egypt and Turkey collapsed and Obama immediately placed sanctions on Egypt. I believe he did that for two reasons. First, the optics of promoting democracy required such action. Second, he was sending a message to Turkey—telling them that they, not Egypt, were the United States' true ally.

My strategy paper with Seth Cropsey is sending a very different message—and getting strange messages back. In 2014, Seth and I traveled to Cyprus for a meeting with the nation's president. We also met the US ambassador to the island, John Koenig. He told us he was looking for help. After that meeting, Seth and I sent emails to the embassy with policy ideas. Once our paper came out, our emails were not returned. Clearly, our policy ideas ruffled feathers. As I'll share later, a former US ambassador told me the State Department didn't like our paper at all.

They didn't like my next move either.

OPENING DOORS

I had made a series of close contacts within the Israeli, Cypriot, and Greek embassies. These will serve me well in the future when I start out on my consulting business. But while the world begins isolating the new Egyptian president, I urge my Greek and Cypriot political contacts to reach out to him. "Go and talk with Egypt," I tell an insider at the Ministry of Foreign Affairs in Athens. "You need to support this government." The response was hesitant at first. "How can we do that?" my associate asks. "He just pulled a coup. That's suicide for us."

"This is a new reality," I say. "You need to make best friends with these people because without them, you don't stand a chance in this part of the world."

Only two members of the European Union attend Sisi's inauguration on June 8, 2014: Cyprus and Greece.

Not long after that, I get my first meeting with the military defense attaché for the US embassy in Athens. He wants to know who I am and what I'm doing.

As embarrassing as it is to admit, it never occurs to me that by doing something I saw as a positive—furthering security and stability for America by promoting a new Mediterranean alliance—I might be creating enemies. Chemistry and physics aren't the only fields where every action causes an equal and opposite reaction. It happens in politics as well. I haven't learned that lesson yet.

When I do, I learn the hard way.

LEVIATHAN RISING

Starting in the summer of 2014, I begin connecting with energy companies interested in working on the pipeline that would theoretically be built by Noble Energy to export gas from Israel. The question is, where would this pipeline go? Noble Energy, a major sponsor of research at the Hudson Institute, had obtained a contract to tap the gas field reserves. Projections for Cyprus's Aphrodite gas field, which basically abutted the Leviathan range, were also very encouraging.

The Obama administration is pushing to develop a pipeline that would deliver these resources to Turkey for distribution throughout Europe. In keeping with my ambition to turn Greece into a closer ally, I push the idea of directing a pipeline there.

Noble is a small operation compared to the players who want in: ExxonMobil, Chevron, BP, Shell. As you can imagine, there is a lot of international interest in the project—especially from the British. That makes sense. The United Kingdom has two army bases on Cyprus and a longstanding connection to Greece and Israel. Australian energy companies also make approaches. My contacts at the Israeli embassy introduce me to a number of figures looking to do business, and I fly to Israel a number of times to represent client interests.

GAZING INTO THE FUTURE

Fast-forward to the summer of 2015, and I've run my course at the Hudson Institute. It is time to move on. I'm about to turn twenty-eight, and I feel like I need to do one of three things: take the plunge and go to law school, get a job in the energy industry, or get some political experience and join a campaign.

On June 16, 2015, I'm at the institute when Donald Trump announces his presidential campaign. I have a gut feeling about Trump at the time, and I announce to the office that I think he has a real chance. Everybody laughs at the idea. "No way," say my beltway insider colleagues, guys who have lived and worked in D.C. for their whole lives. "He doesn't have a prayer."

To my way of thinking Trump is like a stock. In order to profit from it, I have to buy low—in other words, I feel I should offer my services to the campaign immediately. The more Team Trump grows, the harder it's going to be for me to land a gig there. I send an email to Trump's campaign manager Corey Lewandowski offering my services. "I am very interested in leveraging my strong background in policy, energy, and commercial awareness to transition into the Trump campaign team," I write, tooting my own horn a bit.

Corey writes back quickly: "Where are you located? I'd like to connect you to the best possible person within the organization."

I tell him I'm in D.C., and I give him my spiel: Hudson Institute, Greece, Cyprus, Israel, innovative thinker, pro-business, energy connections, relentless networker. He never says yes, but he never says no, either. I keep in contact, sending him updates on what I'm doing, where I'm speaking, what I'm writing.

BACK TO LONDON

In September 2015, I join my good friend Anthony Livanios and a company called Energy Stream, an international outfit that hosts energy conferences in Europe. As I mentioned, I'm crazy about London. I love the collision of different worlds that takes place there: the old venerable institutions and clubs, the innovative business community, the influx of people and cultures from all over the globe.

On October 26, Energy Stream holds the London Oil and Gas Forum, a two-day conference at the Rag Army & Navy Club. Anthony and I had to wrangle a strong list of energy experts, including British Petroleum VP Emily Olson; Kostas Andriosopoulos, vice chairman of Greece's leading natural gas company DEPA; and many political figures and industry players.

One of the bigwigs at the conference is Matthew Bryza, the former US ambassador to energy-rich Azerbaijan. After leaving the State Department, Bryza had settled in Istanbul and began consulting with a number of Turkish energy companies, but the perception among many in the industry was that he operated in lockstep with the American foreign service. When we cross paths at the conference, he seems upset to see me.

"I never thought you would have showed up to this one. What on earth are you doing here?"

There are nicer ways to say hello.

As you can imagine, Bryza is not a fan of my work with the Hudson Institute, and I take his question as an intimidation tactic. He wants to let me know I'm pissing people off in both the State Department and the private sector. The implication is: how dare I show up at a European energy conference! Of course, my vision of Israel and Cyprus working together with Greece completely runs counter to the Obama State Department's grand plans for the Mediterranean—not to mention Bryza and his Turkish clients. So I'm not totally surprised that he sees me as an adversary. And he's not alone: He tells me that the State Department has been highly critical of my work.

Also at the meeting is David Kovatch, the US embassy's director from the Department of Energy. We talk a bit, and he invites me to the embassy to discuss my work and projects. I mention both these meetings because they represent my first inkling that I am on someone's radar. People know who I am and are aware of my policy ideas, which are clearly ruffling the feathers of the political establishment. It also makes me wonder—for the first time in my life—if I am being watched.

I really like Energy Stream, but three months into the job, I am approached by a man named Nagi Khalid Idris who offers me a position at the London Centre of International Law Practice.

Idris is an interesting figure. As it turns out, he is the first in a handful of interesting figures I am about to meet. A Sudanese-born UK citizen, he's the founder of EN Education Group Limited—an education consultancy operation that's core business seems to be placing students from Arab countries in international settings. According to one report, an Arabic version of the company website claimed the company could place students in a number of locales: Thailand, Malaysia, Malta, Russia, Austria, Ireland, New Zealand, Australia, Canada, and the United States. Some of those countries are obvious education and emigration magnets. Others—Malta, Russia, Thailand, and Malaysia—seem a little odd.

Idris is also the founder of the London Centre of International Law Practice. He offers me a great-sounding job: Director of the Centre's International Energy and Natural Resources Division. Despite the organization's name, there is very little law being practiced there. It is essentially a think tank that also offers guidance on international law issues. There is no actual litigation of active legal cases going on there. But the office, located in the middle of Bayswater, an enclave with a large Arab population, generates a lot of international traffic.

So there is a lot of networking going on, but not a lot of interesting policy work. I enjoy meeting with diplomats, going out for dinner and drinks. But in terms of meaningful work, doing deals or engaging in policy discussions, things are on a low boil. Meanwhile, across the Atlantic, a presidential election is looming large. There are a lot of business-as-usual candidates—senators like Marco Rubio and Ted Cruz and governors like Jeb Bush and John Kasich. But I remain very intrigued by Trump. I've kept emailing Corey, waiting, hoping he will hook me up.

CHAPTER 3

CAMPAIGN FEVER

I 'VE ALWAYS HAD a rebellious streak. Even at the Hudson Institute my neoconservative vision was different from that of the resident experts. The idea of uniting Greece, Cyprus, and Turkey as a buffer to Turkey's power in the region flew in the face of accepted wisdom—not just for the security wonks at the institute but with the Obama administration that was in power at the time.

I suppose my interest in upending some of the status quo drew me toward the Trump campaign. Also, I had been an outsider in Washington to a certain degree, so the idea of someone else cracking the exclusive corridors of power was appealing to me.

There were a number of other reasons I was intrigued by the Trump campaign. Just as I had once felt connected to George W. Bush—I was a know-nothing teenager who found Dubya a more relatable, down-to-earth, personable figure than Al Gore—I thought Trump was far more charismatic than Jeb Bush and any of the others pursuing the Republican nomination. I also felt he had an appeal that the media and beltway pundits were ignoring—even though it was hiding in plain sight. Television is the number one campaigning tool in America and has been for decades. Every campaign raises money to spend on TV advertising. That is the number one aim of fundraising. Donor dollars are used to shoot political commercials and then to buy advertising time on TV.

To me, Trump had an enormous advantage in TV exposure. Years before the race began, he had started capturing a significant amount of the electorate's mindshare as the star of *The Apprentice*. It was a hit show! For twelve solid years, starting in 2004, tens of millions of Americans opted to tune in every week. Those were tens of millions of voters who elected *The Apprentice* every week with their TV remotes, choosing to spend time with this character. If that wasn't a bellwether of his viability, I don't know what was.

Look, there is little doubt that Trump is, in some regards, the accidental president. According to sources who joined the early stages of his campaign, he did not expect to win the Republican nomination, much less win the national election. Insiders believe he initially threw his hat in the ring as a low-cost way to extend his brand—to promote his most valuable asset: the Trump name. As far as anyone can tell, that was pretty much his go-to business model before the campaign: he would license his name to anyone who would pay for it. But as the campaign got off the ground, I thought he had a chance, and in late 2015 as I was watching from across the pond, it still seemed very possible.

The election campaign is getting underway, and I keep emailing Corey Lewandowski, letting him know what I'm doing in London, who I'm meeting with.

But in these early days, the campaign is still something of a pipe dream, a lark that is going surprisingly well but not something worth staffing up for. That's what I'm telling myself, anyway. The other candidate catching my eye is another outsider, Dr. Ben Carson. Yes, he is a longshot, but he is the only candidate to ever land ahead of Trump in any of the polls. In fact, in late October a NY Times/CBS poll has Carson beating Trump 26% to 22%, and in early November in 2015 a Wall Street Journal/NBC national poll reports he has a six-point lead over Trump, 29% to 23%. His support is rooted in two things. First, he is the most fervently evangelical candidate in the entire field. Second, he is a Republican African-American who had publicly attacked President Barack Obama. I don't think he has a chance to capture the nomination, but it occurs to me that if Carson drops out and supports Trump, it will be game over as far as the Republican nomination is concerned. Trump wins. And if that happens, being part of Carson's campaign might finally open some doors over at Team Trump.

I shoot an email to the head of the Carson campaign, Barry Bennett, and make my pitch. Is this cynical of me? I like to think it is a strategically smart decision.

The very next day Bennett interviews me via Skype, and I'm hired on as a campaign advisor. One day later, I fly into Baltimore and drive out to the campaign headquarters in Alexandria, Virginia. It is an odd experience for me. All of a sudden, I've gone from wining and dining diplomats and energy experts in London to landing right smack in the middle of Ben Carson's evangelically rooted campaign. I am the total fish out of water, and honestly, the suburban sprawl of Alexandria feels foreign to me after London. Coming from the professional world of London and D.C. think tanks, I show up at the campaign wearing a suit, dressed to the nines. On team Carson, every other person seems to be wearing a cowboy hat. So that is the first surprise.

What catches me off guard next is that every meeting begins and ends with a prayer. This rite, an extension of Ben Carson's persona and his core constituency, is totally alien to me. Although I grew up in a Republican enclave of suburban Chicago, I'd say the community was largely comprised of fiscal Republicans—doctors, lawyers, finance guys. They were very different from the Carson Republicans I am meeting. These are God, heartland, and country types. So it is a useful educational experience for me; I realize I've grown up in bubbles most of my life. My Chicago bubble, my London bubble, my D.C. bubble. So Ben Carson's team, they make me aware of a vast segment of America I'd never experienced, and I'm grateful for that.

Of course, the Carson campaigners inhabited their own bubble. I am as weird to them as they are to me. Bennett introduces me this way: "Hey, guys, this is George Papadopoulos, the Greek guy." I just smile and laugh. But really, it feels demeaning, as if I'm nothing more than a foreigner. Maybe he is trying to celebrate our differences, but I doubt it.

I may have been Bennett's last hire. One week later, he gets the ax, and the campaign falls into disarray. Rumors are floating around that some money had been embezzled from the campaign. That's really bad for morale. A campaign is a complex organism with lots of arms and legs—policymakers, strategists, voter registration teams, finance committees, regional committees—but ultimately it is a team. Nobody's getting rich, except maybe the media experts. Most of the members are working for pennies if they are getting paid at all. So losses—negative media, bad fiscal news, and electoral defeats—they all hurt the team. Dr. Carson tries to keep the campaign afloat.

But the path to the presidency for an African-American evangelical conservative just isn't there.

When he calls it quits, I thank him for a great experience, and I mean it. The campaign has been a fascinating, completely engaging job. I love my work—prepping Dr. Carson for a meeting with Jordan's leaders; helping him prepare for debates; and writing white papers to define the campaign's positions on key issues. It has been high pressured and challenging, and I come away with a much deeper understanding of conservative rural America. These are truly invaluable experiences.

I move back to London and check in with the London Centre of International Law Practice. They seem happy to have me back. As far as Nagi is concerned, my experience working with a US presidential candidate is a feather in the LCILP's cap. Nagi tells people in the office, "George just worked for the Carson campaign. He's very well known in politics. We can use that to generate business."

I am not entirely comfortable with this; the LCILP is a strange operation. Honestly, I'm not entirely sure how or why it exists. And I'm not sure I want to be the poster boy to wrangle new business for a company with such a murky mission. There is still no actual law practice going on that I can see. There are a lot of young, intelligent experts on staff, and there seem to be a number of clients from the Arab world coming into the office. But as far as actual work, it all seems pretty hazy. Eventually, I will discover I am not the only one with questions about the organization.

A SUCCESSFUL CAMPAIGN

In early March of 2016, my overtures to the Trump campaign finally pay off. I email Corey one more time, letting him know I've just finished a stint on the Carson campaign and again offer my services to the Trump team. This time he writes back, putting me in touch with Michael Glassner, executive director of the Donald Trump for President campaign committee. Glassner, who is helping Sam Clovis put together a foreign policy advisory team, forwards my email. Soon after, Clovis himself reaches out, and we schedule a Skype interview. Prepping for the interview, I try to stay calm and tell myself I am still a long shot. Trump's stock is rising now with each primary victory. But I am determined to catch it on the upswing.

Feeling positive and a little cocky, I notify Nagi that it is likely I'll be joining the Trump campaign. Nagi's warm, "you-are-a-star" attitude toward me immediately shifts. "What are you thinking? Why would you do this?" The hostility is palpable and leaves me confused. Is he pissed that I am becoming involved with Trump? Or is he just upset I might be leaving the LCILP? Then another London Centre Director, Peter Dovey, drops by. There is no love from Dovey, either; he rips into me: "This is very bad. You should not be working with Trump. He's a threat to society. He's a racist. He's anti-Muslim."

The next day I'm at my place in London when I have my call with Clovis. It goes better than I could have possibly imagined. We discuss my background. We discuss the rest of the team. He's in a great mood, laughing, kind of giggling, during most of the conversation. Given his girth and gray hair, he strikes me as the Santa Claus of Team Trump.

During the interview, there's a lot of "you're perfect, you're the best guy in the world for what we need." He tells me he thinks my background in the energy business is interesting. And as we discuss international affairs, Russia comes up—though Clovis has since denied saying that the Trump campaign wanted to improve relations with that nation.

At the end of the call, Clovis waxes on about putting together a great team. "You are one of the guys," he says. I'm in though I will be an unpaid advisor—a bit of a disappointment since the Carson team had compensated me pretty well—I shrug it off. I am about to start work on the hottest, most renegade campaign in the country! I had set out to make something happen, and now it was happening. It's a satisfying moment, and I tell myself that if I make valuable contributions to the campaign and Trump wins, I'll land a position with the administration. If not, I'll make some terrific Republican Party connections that will pay off down the road.

I'm making a great investment in my own education and future.

And I'm about to join the team of the likely nominee of the Republican Party. What, I ask myself, is the worst that could happen?

A SUDDEN SHIFT

The next day, I mention my departure to a few colleagues at LCILP. One of them, a water distribution expert from California named Rebecca Peters, starts quizzing me about my motives for joining Team Trump. "Why are you doing this?"

It seems like a ridiculous question. To me the answer is obvious.

"Because it's a presidential campaign!" I say. Then I sigh. It's clear I'm going to have to get used to this reaction from most of the intelligentsia at LCILP.

Then Nagi comes by my office again. His attitude has suddenly changed. It's a night-and-day difference. He starts telling me that there is someone I have to meet, a very important person who will be very useful to me during my time with Trump. I remember Nagi telling me, "He's a man who knows many people." Then he insists I join him at a conference at Link Campus University in Rome.

And he calls in a director with the LCILP whom I've never laid eyes on.

"You have to meet her," he tells me while we wait. "Her name is Arvinder Sambei. She's setting up our team at the conference, and she can help arrange the introduction." She drops by the office for a brief exchange of hellos. I have no idea this frizzy-haired lawyer had prominent positions as senior crown prosecutor and legal adviser to the UK's Ministry of Defence.

And Nagi also fails to tell me that as far back as 2001, she represented the FBI in English court. But I'm getting ahead of myself.

When she leaves, Nagi starts talking about international relations. It is such a radical shift in tone and subject matter from his anti-Trump screed a day earlier that if it were a cartoon, I'd expect to see a light bulb switching on over his head. He starts yammering about all these conversations that he wants the LCILP to be a part of.

"Nagi, I don't have time," I say, reiterating that I'm heading to the United States to join the Trump team.

But he keeps at me, insisting I had to go to Rome. "It's a three-day conference. It will help you with Trump."

Even though I am still completely mystified by the business model and purpose of the LCILP, I feel a slight allegiance to this company. It seems like the least I could do. Also, three days in Rome sounds a bit like a paid vacation. And maybe Nagi, who clearly does have international connections, is telling the truth and I will actually meet people who can help me.

Two years later, when I think about the timing of all this—the sudden focus on Russia right after Sam Clovis had discussed Russia during my interview with him—I wonder if LCILP had recorded the conversation somehow. Or if someone else had and let Nagi know. What else would explain this sudden Russia focus? Or was it all just an innocent coincidence?

SPOOK UNIVERSITY

On the surface, Link Campus University—which bills itself as "the International University of Rome"—is a beautiful school. Located in Quartiere XIII Aurelio near the city center, just over a mile from Vatican City, it is a stunning, cloistered school, with venerable-looking architecture and charming landscapes. Walking the grounds, it feels old and wise.

Its background, as I've since discovered, is less august and academic—and a lot more ominous.

Despite the Renaissance vibe, the school was in fact established in 1999 as the Rome branch of the University of Malta and was the first foreign-owned university authorized to operate in Italy. At some point, it severed ties with the mothership and became a privately owned, for-profit institution.

It also became a training ground for spies, according to reports in the *Washington Post* and *The Epoch Times.* A training school for Western-allied spies, including CIA, FBI, and MI6. The school offered a master's degree in intelligence and security until 2016. It also reportedly offered a master's program in behavioral analysis and applied sciences in intelligence and homeland security.

Offering these fields of study doesn't mean a school is churning out spies. But there is a preponderance of evidence that the school has strong ties to the intelligence community. The university has hosted CIA-sponsored events on campus, including a three-day symposium in 2004, "New Frontiers of Intelligence Analysis," which was attended by intelligence and law enforcement agencies from nearly thirty countries.

Washington Post scribe David Ignatius, who attended the event, reported that the CIA's deputy director for intelligence, Jami Miscik, was a featured speaker. Miscik certainly isn't the only intelligence player to have visited the campus. Former UK Joint Intelligence Committee member Claire Smith was photographed at another Link Campus University conference in 2012. And Andrew Bagley, the future attorney for Crowd-Strike—the cybersecurity firm that traced the 2015 hack of the Democratic National Committee—attended Link Campus in 2010 as a visiting researcher, according to an internet prowling political analyst named Chris Blackburn.

But I didn't know any of this when I went to Rome.

LA VITA ACIDA (THE SOUR LIFE) BEGINS

On March 12, 2016, I arrive at Link Campus with a bunch of colleagues from LCILP, including Donald Lewis, who is a fellow at Stanford University and an expert in Chinese law, Rebecca Peters, and Nagi. The school's general director, Pasquale Russo, gives us a tour. Later, I meet Vincenzo Scotti, the former Italian minister of foreign affairs who also led a crackdown on the mafia when he was the minister of the interior.

Naturally, he has connections to Italian intelligence services. So, right away, I feel good about coming to the conference. Even if nothing else happens, I will meet a few high-level Italian politicians.

I attend a number of sessions, the most memorable for me, given my interests in the Mediterranean and the energy business, being about Italy and its relationship to Libya. The head of a Libyan opposition group was on hand and talking with Italian intelligence officials.

After that session, I'm sitting in a conference room when Nagi Idris approaches. At his side is a well-dressed man in his mid-fifties.

"George," Nagi says. "This is Professor Joseph Mifsud, and you should talk."

Joseph Mifsud is the man Nagi had planned for me to meet, the man Nagi had asked Arvinder Sambei to contact, and the man Nagi had portrayed as a major player, a guy with diplomatic experience and extensive contacts. A man, in other words, who can change my life.

It turns out Mifsud has a PhD in Education from Queen's University, Belfast, which isn't exactly what I'd expect from a guy reputed to be politically connected. But Mifsud spins himself as a worldly insider, a guy with an I-have-connections-everywhere arrogance. He offsets that by flashing warmth and interest in me. He asks about my background. He asks if I have Russian contacts. I shake my head.

"I heard you have connections," I say. "And that you might be able to help me with the campaign."

"Oh yes, absolutely. Let's talk tonight. Let's go to dinner."

There are moments in life when something seismic happens but you don't realize it's happening. This was one of those moments. It occurred during a conference—a place where people are introduced all the time. And it happened in a way that seemed casual.

It was a short meeting. It seemed perfectly natural.

In truth, it was anything but.

Now I wonder if that approach is what's taught in espionage school.

THE SLY PITCH

The evening of March 12, 2016, we meet at a fancy Italian restaurant by the Trevi Fountain—Trattoria al Moro, an old-school, wood-paneled, high-ceiling Roman eatery. We're drinking wine. Mifsud asks me if I'm an Orthodox Christian. It's a strange question on the surface.

Looking back, I think it was a lure, a probe. The Greek Orthodox Church and the Russian Orthodox Church are close cousins. He was looking for some way to bring Russia into the conversation.

When I tell him I'm not particularly religious, he becomes more direct. Am I pro-Russia? Am I hostile to Moscow?

"Look," I say. "I have my contacts. They are mostly in the Middle East. My understanding is that you're connected to Russia."

"Not only Russia, George. I'm very connected everywhere."

"That's interesting," I say, waiting for specifics. I have the impression that to Mifsud this is some kind of a diplomatic dance, and he clearly wants to lead. I wait for more. I don't have to wait long.

"I'm going to be your middleman around the world. I have contacts everywhere. From the State Department to Parliament to Russia, where I've done a lot of work. The Vietnamese president is a good friend of mine, and I should introduce you. I'm very well known."

My initial impression is that I have just hit a gold mine. Think about it. I've just been named a foreign policy advisor. I've just been told Trump wants to improve relations with Russia. And here is someone—a guy I'm under the impression was a former diplomat in his native country of Malta—offering to open the door. If what Mifsud is saying is true, he'll boost my own stature with the campaign and help the campaign itself.

Or so I thought at the time..

Then Mifsud says: "I'm going introduce you to everyone and set up a meeting between Trump and Putin."

"That's an excellent idea," I say. "You really think it can be arranged?"

"Oh, yes. I can do it."

"That would be amazing."

Am I completely naive?

I'm sure some will scoff at my behavior. Everyone's hindsight is 20-20. But my former boss in London told me he would introduce me to a real player. And now that I'd met him, that player sure seems real.

We wrap up dinner, and I go back to my hotel.

On March 14, I send an email to Sam Clovis reporting that I've met Vincenzo Scotti, Italy's former foreign minister, and that I "have also made the acquaintance of some other high-level European policy makers" who can help us in the future.

Mifsud emails me a few days later when I'm back in London to tell me he wants to introduce me to somebody very important. When am I available?

I respond with some possible dates. Then I head to the LCILP offices where I run into Nagi Idris. He's very excited. He tells me I'm going to meet Putin's niece. That Mifsud knows her and is going to introduce us. I'm surprised that he knows more about my future activities than I do. It seems a little bizarre. But I don't dwell on it. The phrase "Putin's niece" is the bigger issue. Could this be true?

Nagi is actually happier than I am. I'll never forget that. "Go meet Joseph!" he cheers. "We'll be waiting here for you."

THE MYSTERY OF PUTIN'S NIECE

The lunch is booked for March 24 at the Grange Holborn Hotel, a luxe London establishment located not far from the British Museum and Russell Square. I put on my best suit for the occasion. I want to make a good impression for the niece of the Russian president. When I get there, Mifsud is waiting for me in the lobby with an attractive, fashionably dressed young woman with dirty blonde hair at his side. He introduces her as Olga Vinogradova. She gives me a warm, charming smile. Then she struggles to apologize about her poor English.

"My Russian is terrible, too." I say. I'm not sure she understood.

As we sit down to eat, I notice a big, burly, bald guy in a leather jacket and jeans keeping a casual gaze on Olga. Is he a bodyguard? I can't be sure. Maybe he is just a guest at the hotel with an appreciative eye and too much time on his hands. Or maybe I'm just too damn watchful.

The lunch turns into another opportunity for Mifsud to spin dreams of deal-making with Russia. Olga remains little more than smiling, nodding table-candy for him; she's basically a great-looking prop in terms of our conversation. In fact, I don't recall her joining the conversation at all. Despite that, Mifsud sells her hard. "Olga is going to be your inside woman to Moscow. She knows everyone." He tells me she was a former official at the Russian Ministry of Trade. Then he waxes on about introducing me to the Russian ambassador in London.

I file all this away. I can't believe my good fortune. It's like I'm living a dream. In less than two weeks, I've joined a campaign, I've glided through a conference of power brokers in Rome, met a super-connected professor who seems to know everyone in Europe, and now I'm meeting a gorgeous Russian woman—the niece of Vladimir Putin, no less—with a hotline to the Kremlin. Everything is elegant, everything is posh and catered. It's so easy. It's like a dream, a movie. Everyone is out of central casting.

We say goodbye, and I go home and immediately fire off another email to Sam Clovis, reporting that Joseph Mifsud, "the director of the London Academy of Diplomacy," introduced me to someone I'm told is "Putin's niece." And since Mifsud had just promised to connect me to the Russian ambassador—a promise, by the way, he never makes good on—I throw in a line about meeting the Russian bigwig, too. After all, Mifsud talks about the ambassador as if a meeting is a done deal. "They are keen to host us in a 'neutral' city, or directly in Moscow," I tell Clovis, and others on the advisory team. I portray Mifsud as a very good friend of mine. And I add that I'm "waiting for everyone's thoughts on moving forward with this very important issue."

"This is most informative," Clovis responds. "Let me work it through the campaign. No commitments until we see how this plays out. We need to reassure our allies that we are not going to advance anything with Russia until we have everyone on the same page. More thoughts later today. Great work."

I was thrilled—especially with the last line—that is just what I want to hear. My goal is to serve the campaign, to open doors,

CHAPTER 4

POWER GAMES

I FLY INTO D.C. on March 30, 2016, and check into the Dupont Hotel. It's the night before my meeting with Trump and the foreign policy advisory team, and I am a jittery bunch of nerves—thanks to jet lag and genuine excitement. I have no idea who will be at the meeting. Trump, obviously, but I assume there will be a fair share of senators, congressmen, and senior military officers. Me? I'm a twenty-eight-year-old from suburban Chicago with three months of campaign experience on the Carson run. *I* know what I've done: my security studies master's degree from University College London, my work with the Hudson Institute, my behind-the-scenes work with Greece and Cyprus regarding Egypt, my work with Israel, all the talks at top energy conferences, and the policy papers I've published. But I'm young. I worry some people will think I'm an outsider crashing their party. Then I think if there's one person who will appreciate that, it's Trump. He's crashing the biggest party of all.

I'm also coming down from my first crazy week in the media spotlight. On March 22, a few days before I flew in, the *Washington Post* broke a story naming five of Trump's foreign policy advisors. My name is on the list, along with Department of Defense Inspector General Joseph Schmitz, Mitt Romney campaign vet Walid Phares, retired Army Lt. Gen. J. Keith Kellogg, and energy consultant Carter Page.

When the article hits, it's exciting, exhausting, confounding, and awesome. Until that moment, I wasn't on the radar of anyone in the media. Now, all of a sudden, my phone is ringing off the hook. Journalists from media outlets around the world call and email me.

The *Post* article itself is a snark attack as far as I'm concerned—even though Trump actually described me as "an oil and energy consultant—excellent guy," according to audiotape the paper eventually released. Instead, the story mocked me for finishing college in 2009 and for having participated in Model UN. I thought that was a low blow, as if my youth were some kind of crime. I also wondered if *Washington Post* reporters would mock other journalists for having written for their college newspapers—how is that any better than Model UN? They are both largely unpaid training endeavors. Things you do to gain experience. So it was a total bush league move.

Unfortunately, it launched what would become a common line of attack against me: I had limited political or policy experience. Actually, I'm pretty sure I had published more articles than some of the "more experienced" gentlemen named in the article. Still, it was easier for reporters Missy Ryan and Steven Mufson to mock me instead of doing any comparative reporting.

On the day of the meeting, I hop out of bed with an anxious smile plastered on my face. Today is the day I'll meet the man dominating the headlines and shaking up the establishment. I shower, shave, and get dressed in record time. I show up early.

The Trump International Hotel, located in the magnificent building that was the Old Post Office, is still being refurbished. When I walk in, the scene is pretty intense: there are Secret Service guys in full body armor. They are running security and checking everyone's I.D. and bags. I make it through and head to the meeting room. There's no breakfast, but there are bowls of Snickers. It's an odd snack, but it fits perfectly with what I know of the candidate's infamous diet—or lack thereof. I grab a campaign Snickers bar.

A bunch of men in their late fifties and sixties are mulling around. Behind me, two guys are talking about Turkey and how they believe that nation is a crucial piece of the geopolitical puzzle. Their voices are overly loud. It's obvious they want me to hear. I turn around. It's Walid Phares and J.D. Gordon.

It seems pretty clear the remarks are directed at me. They're taunting me. Then Phares makes it even more explicit.

"Who's your billionaire father?" he says.

This demeaning question is the first thing anyone says to me? So much for team spirit, right? I laugh and walk away without giving him an answer. Lesson learned. These brilliant strategists had read the *Post* article and made up their minds that I am some rich kid playing politics thanks to my billionaire father's influence with Trump.

If only!

But I get it: This is a small group of competitive people. People looking to curry favor with a man who might be president of the United States. So everyone's sizing each other up, trying to see who has the most to offer, who has the biggest clout. They all want to increase their sphere of influence. They definitely want to squeeze out the young guy who, in their minds, doesn't belong there. I shrug it off.

A Secret Service agent comes in and informs us that Trump will be arriving soon. We line up to greet him. He strides in. I knew he was tall, but he is much taller than I expected. He goes down the line shaking everyone's hand and looking them in the eye. Then we all sit down.

There's a good chance you've seen a picture of this meeting: Ten men sitting at a conference room table, Trump at one end, Jeff Sessions at the other. Remember the *Sesame Street* segment—one of these things is not like the other? That's what I think about when I see this picture. Everyone is in their fifties, sixties, and seventies, except me. Half the room has gray hair or no hair. There's only one guy under the age of thirty and there's only one guy with swarthy skin, and he's the same guy: Me.

But there I am, in the middle of the action.

I love this picture. I'm proud of this picture. It provides proof that I was part of the team. So many people have derided me or claimed I was an underling. Not to get too ahead of the story, but Michael Caputo, who worked briefly on campaign communications, later called me "a coffee boy" while trying to downplay my involvement in the campaign. Do I look like I'm wearing an apron? Caputo, by the way, is the communications genius who couldn't stop himself from tweeting "Ding dong the witch is dead!" after Corey Lewandowski departed from the Trump team. Caputo resigned that very day— June 20, 2016—so how was he in any position to know about my work in the campaign? He wasn't.

I take my seat at the table, and Trump says, "I want to know who everyone is." So we go around the table and introduce ourselves. "Mr. Trump, my name is George Papadopoulos. I've worked at the Hudson Institute and consulted on a number of energy deals in the Mediterranean."

Then Jeff Sessions begins guiding the discussion, bringing up a range of topics. I sit and listen. When foreign policy comes up as a discussion, I perk up. I know I've sent emails about arranging a meeting with Moscow, but I have no idea if any of that information made it to the candidate. I wait to see if Sam Clovis or Michael Glassner say anything since Sam and I have discussed a Russian meeting, and I figured that he had consulted with Glassner. But nobody mentions it. Maybe there's a whole groupthink going on that so often infects Washington neoconservatives, and nobody wants to say anything. So this is it; this is the time to make my pitch.

"I've been in contact with people in Europe who are eager to set up a meeting for you with Russia. And I can make it happen," I say.

The room is silent. I look across the table. Michael Glassner shifts from this slightly surprised look on his face—a kind of, "Wow, you really had the balls to say that in this crowd?"—to a poker face. Vince Carafano, a cold warrior from the Heritage Foundation, is shaking his head as if he hates the idea.

I look at a couple of other people. Some are nodding, maybe in approval, but it's hard to tell; there's no chorus of "amens." It would be nice to have an ally, but I don't really care. There are only two people whose opinions matter: Trump, obviously, and Sessions, the most senior government figure in the room.

I look at Trump. He nods noncommittally, as if he's processing the idea. "What do you think, Jeff?" he asks.

"It's a good idea. We should look into this."

OPERATION: MAKE AN IMPACT!

I leave the meeting feeling like a world-beater. Not only had I floated the idea of a Russia meeting but Trump looked very interested, and I perceived Jeff Sessions's reaction as very positive. I said something that caught the attention of everyone in the room. And now I was going to make it happen.

Sessions wasn't the only one who seemed to approve. Stephen Miller was also at the meeting, hanging back, the only other young guy in the room. Now, Miller is known as the guy who spearheaded Trump's immigration policies, which appealed to a large segment of the Republican base. But at this time, he's new to the team, too, having been brought on by Sessions.

He comes up to me right after the meeting and shakes my hand. "This sounds promising," he tells me. "Please keep in contact with me. I can run things through to Jeff."

In my head, this is just another in a string of triumphs. From meeting Mifsud and "Putin's niece" now to meeting Trump and his closest advisors, I'm making a name for myself. I'm feeling more motivated than ever to leave an indelible mark on this campaign and, if Trump becomes president, land a role in the administration. That is my thought process. And you know what? I bet every single other person at the meeting had a similar goal.

The next day I fly to Israel to speak at an energy policy conference along with the Obama administration's shaggy-haired former US energy secretary Ernest Moniz. I meet with Eli Groner—my old friend from the Israeli embassy who, at the time, is the director general of the Prime Minister's Office for Benjamin Netanyahu.

I've spoken at other conferences. But this is the first time I can remember people pulling out their phones to take my picture. Although I initially signed up to speak as George Papadopoulos, consultant, now I was also representing the Trump campaign. After the conference, I'm invited to talk with the Begin-Sadat Center for Strategic Studies, a major Israeli think tank. There, I meet David M. Weinberg, who writes an April 7 column about me for the *Jerusalem Post*.

Obviously, I make sure the campaign is okay with my speaking on behalf of Trump. I get the thumbs-up; in fact, I get more than a thumbs-up. The feedback is extremely positive. People are impressed not only that I am making Russia contacts but that I'm also connected in Israel. When Weinberg asks me about Trump's policy stance on Israel and a recent remark about Israel needing to "pay" for its aid from the United States, I immediately launch sound bites to walk that back while moving forward. "Donald Trump is absolutely committed to maintaining Israel's qualitative military edge as a cornerstone of American policy and US-Israel relations," I tell him. "Israel needs and deserves this." I also stress that Trump will work closely with Egypt, Israel's primary ally in the Middle East.

Weinberg asks me about relations with Russia. So I lay out some talking points. I tell him Trump is open to engaging with Russia on a range of common concerns and that the candidate sees Putin as a potential partner. I point out that China is the real superpower threat and that working with Russia to counter Chinese expansionism in Asia and the Middle East is vital. Finally, I stress that both countries are invested in stopping the export of radical and violent Islam from the Middle East and that I thought, if nothing else, Trump and Putin would join forces on that.

From a personal standpoint, the best thing about the article may have been that it described me as a "young, impressive energy expert." I'm not flagging this to toot my own horn. But within the campaign, where optics are of enormous importance, appearance—that is, how you appear to the electorate and the media—is paramount. So this article, presenting Trump as a total Israel supporter, tough on radical Islam, and wary of China while open to Russia, was entirely in sync with campaign goals. It was a win all around.

PAGE TURNS

I'm back in London. It's April 5, and Carter Page reaches out to me. He didn't attend the March 31 meeting. But we'd been CC'd on various campaign emails, so he had my information. I know very little about him, other than that he was the managing partner of something called Global Energy Capital. But we are on the same team, so I figure, great, let's compare notes on Skype. But it's less a talk than a brief lecture.

"Be very careful about talking about Russia," he tells me. "Don't act so confident about making this happen." There is often a fine line between warning someone and threatening him. This felt more like a threat than a warning. Like, if I kept pursuing what campaign bosses had told me they were interested in, I'd be in trouble.

I'm thinking: What the hell is this guy going on about? Why is he trying to order me around when he's a colleague of mine?

"Carter," I say, "I don't know what you're talking about. But I'm just going with what my contacts are telling me, and that's that we can do this."

He doesn't like my response and remains hostile. When we hang up, I wonder if I had stepped on his turf. I report the conversation to Sam Clovis. He tells me to ignore Page and confirms my impression that he is a weird guy with no real influence in the campaign. The world would discover a lot about Carter Page in the future.

We now know that he lived in Moscow between 2004 and 2007. We know that court documents show that Victor Podobnyy, an alleged Russian intelligence operative in New York City, tried to recruit Page as an intelligence source in 2013 and reportedly labeled him an "idiot." We know that three months after his phone call to me, he traveled to Russia and met senior allies to President Vladimir Putin, including Russian deputy prime minister Arkady Dvorkovich. We also know that he once described himself as an "informal adviser" to the Kremlin and that the Steele Dossier—the controversial document on Trump's suspicious links to Russia assembled by former senior British intelligence officer Christopher Steele—alleges that Page served as an intermediary between the campaign and Russian officials eager to see Trump in the Oval Office. And finally, we know that he was suspected of being a Russian intelligence asset—so much so that an October 2016 FBI surveillance application said: "The FBI believes that Page has been collaborating and conspiring with the Russian government."

Page has consistently denied being a Russian agent. But there does seem to be a preponderance of disturbing evidence against him. I still wonder about why, exactly, he reached out to me. Did he want to control who Trump would speak to if any contact with Russia occurred? Was that his motive—to push me out of arranging any Russia talks?

I still don't know the answer.

JEFF SESSIONS

Another thing I don't know is why Jeff Sessions characterized our advisory meeting in his congressional testimony the way he did. I don't want to get too ahead of my story, but about eighteen months after our meeting, Sessions testified before a House Judiciary Committee hearing on oversight of the Justice Department on Capitol Hill on November 14, 2017.

When asked if he had shut down my proposal to reach out to Russia, Sessions, during the Committee hearing serving as the US Attorney General, responded: "Yes, I pushed back."

But a subsequent report by Reuters confirms my version of the events. Three people who attended the meeting—none of whom have any allegiance to me, as far as I know—affirmed that Sessions raised absolutely no objections to my idea. Zero. One source described Sessions as courteous to me. A second said, "It was almost like, 'Well, thank you, and let's move on to the next person.'"

Reuters found one person who claimed Sessions wasn't fibbing. But consider the source: It was J.D. Gordon, the same guy who was taunting me along with Walid Phares before the policy advisors meeting had even started. As a former naval officer and a Pentagon spokesman under George W. Bush, Gordon, who served as the campaign's director of national security, was a hawk when it came to most things Russian. I say "most things" because it turns out Gordon was very friendly with Maria Butina, the Russian gun-rights activist who has copped a plea deal and admitted working to infiltrate Republican political circles and influence US relations with Russia before and after the 2016 presidential election. Gordon, as has been widely reported, was so enamored by the red-haired Russian that he invited her to attend a concert by the rock band

Styx in Washington, D.C., and later he asked Butina to attend his birthday party.

So the only person supporting Jeff Sessions's account about shutting down a Russia meeting is a defense expert who pals around with an admitted Russian operative, did damage control for the Iraq War, and gave me a hard time before he even met me.

He's also a guy who, at the time he made his remark, might have been wondering if he would face any legal trouble for consorting with a suspected spy. I'd want to land on the right side of the man in charge of the DOJ, too.

Of course, at the time, I don't anticipate any backlash or double-talk from that March 31 meeting. I know I'm swimming with sharks, but I feel confident, like I'm sharp enough to navigate the waters, and I'm laser-focused on helping the campaign. Despite Sessions's subsequent attempt to rewrite history, the fact is, I have my marching orders. I am ready to stand and deliver—with the help of Professor Mifsud and Putin's mysterious niece.

CHAPTER 5

TARGET PRACTICE

B ACK IN LONDON in the beginning of April, I finally cut
the cord with the London Centre of International Law Policy. I'm working out of my apartment, which I don't mind. I've
been traveling to D.C. and Israel for a full week, so I'm happy
to stay in and work the phones and email during the day. I have
a lot of catching up to do, both for my consulting business and
for the campaign. I email Professor Mifsud, eager to pick up
where we left off and start solidifying contacts with Russia.

I have to be patient. That's the frustrating thing. I'm dependent on him for introductions. I don't want to seem too pushy.
But I am extremely eager to move ahead.

I email Olga, the woman introduced to me as Putin's niece.
I also email Mifsud asking about arranging "a potential foreign policy trip to Russia" for Trump.

Olga emails me back. Or perhaps I should say a woman claiming to be Olga or posing as Olga emails me back. Her emails are
instantly suspicious—because they are written in perfect English. The woman I'd met at lunch could barely get past "hello."

Now she's sending me emails saying, "I would be very pleased to support your initiatives between our two countries."

The vocabulary and style stun me. I don't know what to think. I wonder if she is using some kind of translation application, like Google Translate, and writing her email in Russian and then cutting-and-pasting the English version to send to me.

But I also wonder if someone else is writing these letters.

I decide to wait and see how she and Mifsud would move the process forward. Mifsud writes: "This is already been agreed (sic). I am flying to Moscow on the 18th for a Valdai meeting, plus other meetings at the Duma." Mifsud is referring to a conference held by the Valdai Discussion Club, a group founded by a think tank called the Russian International Affairs Council which is funded by Russia's Ministry of Foreign Affairs. The Duma is the Russian Congress.

A day later, on April 12, "Olga" writes: "I have already alerted my personal links to our conversation and your request. The embassy in London is very much aware of this. As mentioned, we are all very excited by the possibility of a good relationship with Mr. Trump. The Russian Federation would love to welcome him once his candidature would be officially announced."

So I have no choice but to hurry up and wait. I communicate this back to the campaign managers, primarily Stephen Miller.

A STRANGE INTERLUDE

One of the things about working from home is that, when the evening comes, I don't feel guilty about taking advantage of the city's great nightlife—the pubs, the fine clubs, the great restaurants.

One of my London contacts is an Israeli diplomat named Christian Cantor. At the time, his title is political counselor at the Israeli embassy in London. We sometimes meet for beers at a pub in Bayswater and discuss politics. One evening out, he tells me the Israeli government is terrified of Trump. I find this surprising. He doesn't say why. But he also makes clear to me that in his opinion somebody like Ted Cruz would have been a better Republican candidate because he was more predictable, which I take to mean more evangelical—a demographic that is extremely pro-Israel.

We have a good time. I leave thinking Christian is almost a friend, although it turns out I should've been thinking: watch your back.

DROPPING THE BOMB

I get another email from Olga. It's written in perfect English. I can't believe it. Finally, I have to ask the question that's been on my mind for a few weeks: "Is this the same person who I had lunch with at the Grange Holborn Hotel?"

She never writes back.

On April 18, Mifsud, who is supposedly in Russia at his high-level meetings, introduces me by email to a man named Ivan Timofeev, who is the program director at the Russian International Affairs Council. Apparently, he is in charge of the Valdai conference that Mifsud is attending. Timofeev tells me he has connections at the Ministry of Foreign Affairs, which makes sense considering the ministry funds his entire operation. At one point, Timofeev suggests that we "meet in London or in

Moscow." I say London would be preferable, as I didn't have a travel budget. I also think it would be great to involve the Russian ambassador to the United Kingdom—a connection Mifsud had promised to make and so far failed to deliver on.

The back and forth with Timofeev is encouraging to me. He's the first, really the only, Russian I've ever been in contact with besides the enigmatic Olga. I emailed my contacts at campaign headquarters: "The Russian government has an open invitation by Putin for Mr. Trump to meet him when he is ready. The advantage of being in London is that these governments tend to speak a bit more openly in 'neutral' cities."

Then Mifsud returns from the Valdai conference. On April 26 we meet for breakfast at the Andaz Hotel, near Liverpool Street Station, one of the busiest train stations in London. He's in an excellent mood and claims he met with high-level Russian government officials. But once again, he's very short on specifics. This is becoming a real pattern with Mifsud. He hasn't offered any names besides Timofeev. Then, he leans across the table in a conspiratorial manner. The Russians have "dirt" on Hillary Clinton, he tells me. "Emails of Clinton," he says. "They have thousands of emails."

I don't know what this means. Emails? What kind of emails? Revealing what? As an American citizen, I'm horrified. I'm all for Trump succeeding, but the idea that the Russians would have hacked into the accounts of the former secretary of state and US senator—if that is what he is saying—is unthinkable. Imagine if she were to win the presidency and the Russians had information that they could use against her! I didn't say anything. I am trying to process the information. I wonder if Mifsud is even a remotely reliable source? The whole dance with Olga seems to be nothing more than a scam. Six weeks after our initial meeting, I've been in contact with two Russians, and only one of them seems vaguely close to opening a communications channel for Trump.

But I have to face the facts. Mifsud is all I've got in terms of connecting with the Russians and making good on my reports to the campaign. I've painted myself into a corner, so I've got to stick with him, hope he comes through and figure my way out. So I don't ask about the emails. I don't want to know, really. I don't really care. My mission is to make a meeting happen. End of story. Hacking, security breaches, potential blackmail—that is illegal and treasonous. I want no part in it. I don't pursue the subject, and Mifsud and I return to the one theme that I've been focused on for the campaign, getting concrete next steps out of the professor. But when we say goodbye, I have a feeling he's still just spinning me.

It's no secret that politics and diplomacy require dancing with partners you may otherwise detest. The enemy of your enemy is your friend, according to the old geopolitical saw. But sometimes the enemy of your enemy can be an evil bastard, too. Mifsud, it turns out, was a man with a long and suspect track record. According to a BBC report, the professor worked at a university in Slovenia where he departed amid a scandal over $48,000 in expenses. He was involved in a now shuttered London Academy of Diplomacy. The article, which calls Mifsud the "selfie king of the diplomatic circuit" for his pictures with British bigwigs, reports that although he had a six-month stint working "for the private office of the Maltese foreign minister, he was never a diplomat."

If I'm guilty of anything, it's of not vetting him carefully and of trusting my old employers at the London Centre of International Law Practice when they vouched for him. I should have done better. But at that point, like a gambler who doubles down to recover losses, I felt like I had to keep investing in him.

I write emails expressing my gratitude for his help. I tell him that if we can pull off a meeting, it will be historical—something I truly believe. And I keep updating the campaign.

As for Mifsud's explosive claim that the Russians had the emails of Trump's greatest rival for the presidency?

I don't tell a soul. Not yet, anyway.

BACK TO REALITY

Joseph Mifsud and Ivan Timofeev aren't my only email pals. Stephen Miller and I have been assigned to work on Trump's first foreign policy speech, scheduled for May 1 at the Center for National Interest. Stephen gets the broad outline from the team, and then he and I bang out drafts and email them back and forth.

The speech was upsetting to many in the international community, as Trump accused our allies of "not paying their fair share," declared they "must contribute toward their financial, political, and human costs…of our tremendous security burden," and ripped into Obama's Iran deal.

I am quite proud of some sections, like this one, which features a few Trump ad-libs:

We went from mistakes in Iraq to Egypt to Libya, to President Obama's line in the sand in Syria. Each of these actions has helped to throw the region into chaos and gave ISIS the space it needs to grow and prosper. Very bad. It all began with a dangerous idea that we could make Western democracies out of countries that had no experience or interests in becoming a Western democracy.

We tore up what institutions they had and then were surprised at what we unleashed. Civil war, religious fanaticism, thousands of Americans killed, lives wasted. Horribly wasted. Many trillions of dollars were lost as a result. The vacuum was created that ISIS would fill.

That's an accurate summation of US foreign policy missteps from the Bush administration onward. Every word of it is, unfortunately, true and deserves to be said. We need to own our mistakes.

I bring up all of this for two reasons. First, the speech was one of my most tangible contributions to the campaign. It's been reported that I "edited" the speech. I actually am the coauthor. Second, it's more proof that I was well thought of within the campaign and disproves the false narrative that I was some kind of gopher, or that I, as Trump would later claim, "didn't have much to do with the campaign." That is a total lie. I contributed to policy shaping, filed frequent updates, gave interviews as a campaign surrogate, and helped broker meetings with international leaders. I have hundreds of emails to prove it, too.

AN INNOCENT DATE?

Two days after the speech I get a phone call from Christian Cantor, my acquaintance at the Israeli embassy in London.

"George," he says. "I want to introduce you to my girlfriend."

"Okay. That sounds great," I say. "Who's your girlfriend? What's her name?"

"Erika Thompson."

I've never heard of her. "Great," I say. "I can't wait to meet her."

That evening we meet at the pub. Erika is a pleasant-looking Australian woman in her mid-thirties. She's introduced to me as a member of the Australian High Commission (that's Britspeak for embassy), where she's an assistant to Alexander Downer, the High Commissioner (that's Britspeak for ambassador). And guess what? She is no fan of Trump. "He's a menace," she says. "He'll be a pariah. No one will ever take him seriously. Downing Street hates him."

On and on she goes: "Obviously this guy's not going to win, but if he does, just so you understand, the world is going to coalesce against him." I couldn't believe I was getting lambasted like this. I'm just a policy advisor. I'm the energy guy, the Mediterranean guy. I'm not bullying our allies. But I guess I am Trump-by-proxy. A stand-in. It comes with the territory.

FRONT-PAGE NEWS

A few days later, on May 3, I get a call from none other than the political editor of the *Times of London*, Francis Elliott. He wants to interview me. At the time, I really have no experience with newspapers or reporters. "Sure," I say, being the unguarded advisor. "That would be terrific."

We go to a very chic Italian restaurant in Oxford Circus. Elliott, a guy in his 40s, with a slightly squashed face, cowrote British Prime Minister David Cameron's biography, *Cameron: Practically a Conservative*. According to the *Times* website, he's also in charge of the paper's "trusted, non-partisan, informed, and revelatory political coverage." I figure he's a reliable, straight-shooter. When he asks if he can record me, I say sure.

For the next two hours, we talk about a wide range of political and personal issues. He wants to know if I have family connections to Cyprus, where the British have a lot of interest. I tell him no, my family is Greek, and I'm American. He asks what I'm advising Trump on. I say, everything. We discuss the Iran nuclear deal, trade issues between the United States and the United Kingdom, and the United States relations with China. He also asks me about Brexit—perhaps the most existential concern in all of the United Kingdom. Everything about the interview is going smoothly, I think. There are no real gotcha questions. There's some hostility from Elliott regarding Trump. But it's mild compared to some of the batterings I've taken. As the lunch winds down, I feel pretty good about the whole thing.

Remember, this is early May 2016. Just a few months earlier, on December 16, 2015, British Prime Minister David Cameron, addressing Trump's statements about immigration restrictions, made international headlines saying: "I think his remarks are divisive, stupid, and wrong." Now I'm having lunch with the man who cowrote the first biography of the Tory leader. I should have put two and two together and been on my guard.

The lunch is over. But Elliott has one more question. Just one after our two-hour lunch. "Do you think, George, David Cameron should apologize for making those remarks about Donald Trump?"

As I remember it, my remarks are pretty even-handed. I tell Elliott that I thought it was unbecoming of any sitting prime minister to talk in those terms about any candidate of a foreign country, especially the United States, and that he shouldn't interfere in the political process of another country.

At 1:01 a.m., my words as reported by Elliott have taken on a lot more weight. Splashed on the front page of the *Times* website is a screaming headline:

SAY SORRY TO TRUMP OR RISK SPECIAL RELATIONSHIP, CAMERON TOLD

Elliott had asked me if he could tape our conversation. I have no way of knowing if he got this part of the talk on tape. But his story contains stronger words than I recall using. Here's Elliott's written record of what I said:

"It would seem that if Prime Minister Cameron is serious about reaching out, not only to Mr. Trump's advisors but to the man himself, an apology or some sort of retraction should happen.

"It's unfortunate that Prime Minister Cameron was one of the most outspoken critics of Mr. Trump. Not even the Chinese premier came out with negative statements, or other European leaders," Mr. Papadopoulos said. "To see Mr. Cameron come out as the most vocal opponent was uncalled for. Considering that we believe that the UK-US relationship should be a cornerstone not just of NATO policy but elsewhere it would be wise for him to reach out in a more positive manner to Mr. Trump."

According to this quote, I never explicitly say what the headline suggests—that Cameron needed to apologize to prevent jeopardizing the US-UK alliance. I wasn't issuing a "do this, or else" threat. I would never do that. But that didn't stop Elliott from using my words to spin the most sensationalized interpretation possible.

I am now officially front-page news, and I am not happy about that. Neither, it seems, are some of the people in the campaign. I get an email from Sam Clovis saying, "George, you are in real hot water with the campaign over your comments to the British press. You need to call asap. No more discussion with any press until you hear otherwise or have spoken to me about your current situation." Clovis tells me that some people are very pissed off at me and want my head handed to me. But he also says that he has my back. I thank him for that. Then I email Hope Hicks, Trump's communications director, to let her know that I never gave an ultimatum to the British prime minister. I also tell her that I'm hearing I might be fired and I ask if she can let me know what's up and if Trump is okay with the story.

She emails me back: Trump is fine with this. Don't worry about it.

I'm completely relieved. According to Hope, Trump basically saved my job!

WINING & DINING ON THE CIA

I decide to stay off the radar for a while. But the next day, two military attachés at the US embassy in London, Terrence Dudley and Gregory Baker, reach out to me to set up a meeting. It seemed a little strange to me that two military men were contacting me. But not too strange. While most embassy staff are, in fact, working on behalf of the State Department, it is common knowledge in diplomatic communities that many embassy employees designated as "diplomats" are, in fact, intelligence operatives affiliated with the CIA or military intelligence divisions. I guess someone in Washington—at the State Department, CIA, or the Pentagon—sent a cable: Who is this guy Papadopoulos? Check him out. Was it part of something sinister or just standard operating procedure intelligence gathering? I have no idea.

They take me to a private club known far and wide as The Rag—the same place we hosted the 2015 Energy Stream Conference. Its real name is The Army and Navy Club, and it's located in London's tony Mayfair district. It's been a haunt for well-heeled military men since 1837. The restaurant is lined with portraits of dashing members of the British armed forces. The library is lined with military books. And the bar is lined, of course, with fine whiskeys. I'm not sure which of my hosts is a member of this private club, which costs a minimum of $600 a year in membership fees. But if I had to guess, it would be Dudley. His title is Director, US Navy and Marine Programs, US Office of Defense Cooperation. So it makes sense he'd want to hoist a few cocktails with other military men. But I walk in thinking, how do government officials afford this? My conclusion? These guys must be intelligence operatives with a slush fund or expense account.

They spare no expense during our meeting, dropping at least $500. They ask me what I'm doing in London. "We know all about your work in the Mediterranean and the energy industry and what you were promoting," Dudley says, adding, "I wrote my thesis on energy in the Caucasus." Then Gregory Baker starts speaking Greek to me. "I'm just letting you know, I was stationed in Thessaloniki." That's the city my family is from. He was hitting close to home. Was all this a small-world coincidence, or was I being stalked? I got a little spooked.

The conversation shifts to Russia. They come across as being behind the idea of reaching out to Russia, as if they are parroting Trump's previous remarks. I wonder, given my outreach to Mifsud and Timofeev, if these questions are related to my campaign project. But I also think about Trump's recent speech. He had left a door open to Moscow, saying, "We desire to live peacefully and in friendship with Russia and China. We have serious differences with these two nations and must regard them with open eyes, but we are not bound to be adversaries. We should seek common ground based on shared interests."

Was that speech why two embassy officers were drinking with me and trying to uncover the campaign's perspective on Russia? Was it the article in the *Times of London*? Did one of the cold warriors at the policy group meeting give my name to the State Department, the CIA, or the FBI—and these guys were part of an intelligence-gathering operation? Maybe the answer was all of the above.

Let's flash forward for a moment. In September 2018, more than two years after our tête-à-tête, Dudley and Baker gave an interview claiming they had reached out to me out of personal curiosity. "We approached him from a more fascinated stand-point trying to figure out what his game was," Dudley says. "Who's funding him to be here [in London]? How does he actually get away with doing that?"

In the interview, Dudley also says he thought I was "a naive guy who got in over his head." This is a very interesting comment when you consider that I continued to meet with these guys after that first outing. They took me out for dinner. And at one point one of them even told me that I was "a perfect guy to work for intelligence." They also insisted that if and when I go to Greece, I make contact with the army attaché of the US embassy in Greece. I think that's kind of strange. But I say, sure, tell me his name.

For someone they dismiss as "in over his head," they sure kept tabs on me. They even tried to ingratiate themselves into the campaign, asking if I would get them a job and messaging me up until the inauguration.

MEANWHILE IN AMERICA

The Indiana Republican primary takes place on May 3, 2016. At this point, there are only three potential candidates left standing. And two of them, Ted Cruz and John Kasich, are in dire need of a momentum-swinging miracle to stop the Trump juggernaut. But there are no miracles in sight. Trump crushes his rivals in the primary, winning 53.26% of the vote and all 57 of the state delegates. The delegate count is now a done deal; with only nine other state primaries left, there is no way for the also-rans to catch up. By May 4, Cruz and Kasich have called it quits.

What does that mean for me? I can't lie: it feels good—I invested in Trump. I bet on him when I joined the campaign. I thought he would capture the imagination and faith of Joe & Linda Mainstreet. And I was right. All my colleagues at the Hudson Institute who had laughed at me—many of whom I respected as savvy D.C. insiders—were now proven wrong. The vast majority of the political establishment all over the world was, too.

So, yes, I feel vindicated and energized. And so does the rest of the campaign team. How could we not?

As for the keepers of the flame of status quo—there is a huge amount of hand-wringing and fear. What do our allies think about Trump's "America First" policy that looms in the future? What do our allies who have grown accustomed to America playing the policeman of the world think of his isolationism and his protectionist tariff-rattling? What do our own State Department and intelligence services think? They track world events; they are committed to furthering American interests abroad. But here is a guy threatening to withdraw from our role as an international force for good.

Trump supporters may not realize the level of anxiety their candidate has provoked. I hear it every day while talking to foreign diplomats. There is a profound level of panic out there—abroad and at home. Intelligence operatives are panicking, too. And some of them, I would come to find out, are gearing up to take action.

A FATAL DATE

What was I up to in early May 2016? The same old, same old. But the interest in me keeps increasing, as Trump's candidacy ascends. I'm Mr. Popular all of a sudden. I get yet another invite via email on about May 6. It's from Erika, the Australian "diplomat" who is "dating" the Israeli "political officer" Christian Cantor.

Yes, those quotation marks are there for a reason. A high-profile reporter based in Washington recently told me that Christian and Erika were both intelligence officers for their respective countries, something Erika has repeatedly denied. As for their coupledom, as of September 2018, the pair were reportedly engaged. Congratulations, Mr. & Mrs. Smith!

Erika tells me again that she's Alexander Downer's senior advisor, and that she thinks it is imperative that I meet with him. The upshot is that Downer is exceptionally well connected and that he's eager to get acquainted.

We set up a date for the three of us at Kensington Wine Rooms. It's a very trendy London spot, and a fitting one, I guess, because I seem to be a big trend in the London diplomatic world.

But I ain't seen nothing yet.

CHAPTER 6

THE DEVIL FROM DOWN UNDER

I T'S A WET, ugly London evening on May 10, 2016, when I go meet Erika Thompson and her boss, Australian High Commissioner Alexander Downer.

How appropriate.

As I walk through the rain to The Kensington Wine Rooms, which is about ten minutes from my apartment, I have no idea that this meeting—probably more than any other—will change my life. In the space of less than an hour, a promising, well-intentioned adventure will turn into a long-running nightmare that will destroy my career, my finances, and strain relations with the people I care about the most—my own family.

But there's no reason on earth I should anticipate an impending disaster. Erika has pitched the evening as a friendly get-together to talk about US-Australian relations.

I am not very impressed by the Wine Rooms. For all the buzz about offering 150 different wines by the glass and a name that suggests a sprawling, clubby atmosphere, the eatery is nothing more than a modern restaurant with lots of mechanized wine dispensers. What's the big deal?

I check my phone when Erika emails me. They are running late. I survey the crowd. It's relatively young, well-scrubbed, and prosperous. I study the wine list, which is, on second thought, somewhat impressive. Finally, Erika arrives with this tall, bespectacled gentleman. Maybe it's his big glasses, but he reminds me of a stretched-out, gray-haired version of New Wave popstar Elvis Costello. He sits down, squeezing in at the small table, and Erika makes the introductions, but her manner is formal and distant.

Downer is oozing aggression by comparison. After our introduction, the first thing he says is, "Tell your boss he needs to leave my friend David Cameron alone, and you should leave him alone too."

I'm stunned by this senor diplomat's bullying manner. I've had warmer greetings from ex-girlfriends. So much for Erika's friendly get-together.

"I don't know what you are talking about," I respond. "No one is bothering your friend David Cameron. But he might want to show some respect to the man who is likely to be the next US president."

Downer says nothing. Instead he takes his phone and holds it straight up, as if filming me. But he doesn't really look at the screen. Instead, he's glaring at me. It's a look of scorn. He brings the phone down, but a few seconds later he repeats the move again.

A waiter comes by. Erika orders a round of gin and tonics.

Downer starts talking: He tells me he's connected to a British security firm called Hakluyt. He boasts about being a board member and that the firm has a great presence in London and close ties to the Obama administration. "We advise many governments," he says.

I nod. I'm not sure what to say about this. He shifts gears:

"George, I used to be the UN envoy to Cyprus, and what you are talking about in Cyprus is wrong, and it's a threat to British interests."

British interests? David Cameron? A private British security firm? Isn't this guy supposed to be representing Australian interests? I'm wondering if this guy is all there. So far, he's taken out his phone more times than he's mentioned relations between our two countries.

"I know all about your work in the Middle East and the energy business, and you're wholeheartedly wrong in your assessment. You know the Turks deserve the north of Cyprus," he says. "The energy fields in Cyprus and Israel—Turkey should be the gateway for that energy and not Greece."

I can't believe this. I'm sitting with the Australian High Commissioner, and he's determined to critique my previous policy work, tell me he's well-connected to intelligence operatives, and talk about British interests.

The phone comes out again. He must have grabbed it and held it up at least four times. He is so aggressive, so hostile, it's actually a bit intimidating. I think about saying something, calling him on his bizarre camera work, but I don't want to inflame him further. I want him to calm down, and I want to get the hell away from him. He's the most inappropriate diplomat I've ever encountered.

He tells me he's very pro-Clinton, and he hates Obama.

"That's interesting," I say.

"Obama is an uppity, arrogant guy," he says, a comment that I sense carries racial undertones. Why is this diplomat telling me he's a big fan of Hillary Clinton while ripping America's sitting president—the same president who hired Clinton as his secretary of state? Again, I'm stunned by how unprofessional and hostile Downer is. I feel like I'm being attacked, lectured, and talked down to. I finish my drink. I'm ready to leave.

And then something happens.

Or more accurately, *Downer later claims something happens.*

In his version of events, he asks me a question about Russia and Trump.

I then tell him that the Russians have a surprise or some damaging material related to Hillary Clinton.

I have no memory of this. None. Zero. Nada.

In my version of events, Downer brusquely leaves me and Erika at the table, and we go our separate ways. I remember feeling completely disappointed by the meeting and pissed off about being treated so rudely.

Downer's version, however, is the one that matters.

But that version is quite murky. The High Commissioner has contradicted himself numerous times about the event and failed to answer pointed questions about whether he was spying on me. Some reports stated he spoke directly with the US deputy chief of mission at the US embassy in London, Elizabeth Dibble, about our meeting. Later, I would find out that Dibble was in close touch with embassy operatives Gregory Baker and Terrence Dudley, who were monitoring me as well.

The most widely reported sequence of events is that within forty-eight hours of our meeting, Downer sends a cable to Australian intelligence reporting my alleged remark.

With that single act, he upends my life.

LOOKING AHEAD AND BEHIND

Fast-forward to early 2019: I don't remember Downer asking me a question about the Russians. I have searched my memory repeatedly, trying to remember this exchange. Each time I come up with nothing.

I still don't know the specific remark Downer attributed to me. The contents of the cable he sent to his superiors in Canberra remain a mystery. What did he quote me as saying? In a 2018 interview with an Australian newspaper, he revealed I never used the words "dirt" or "emails" in my alleged remarks about Clinton and Russia.

"He didn't say dirt," Downer told the paper. "He said material that could be damaging to her. No, he said it would be damaging. He didn't say what it was."

I've been told by sources with Congressional ties that Downer was recording our conversation, that there is a transcript. Why would an Australian diplomat record my conversation? Does this prove my allegation that he was illicitly spying on me? Why me? If I did say something about damaging material, I have no memory of doing so. But this happened more than two years ago. Despite what you see in the movies, on TV, or read in nonfiction books, recalling specific conversations is not easy. At any rate, two months after my run-in with Downer, when WikiLeaks began posting emails stolen from the Democratic National Committee by Russian hackers, Australian intelligence reportedly notified US intelligence operatives about Downer's report claiming I said the Russians had damaging goods on Clinton.

Looking back at our meeting, it seems clear that he steered the conversation around to Hillary. Was it intentional? Did this man with extensive intelligence ties already know what Joseph Mifsud—a man who taught at the spook-training ground that is Link Campus Rome—had told me? Was he trying to bait me into saying something? Something that could spark an investigation? I believe so.

Media reports—starting with the *New York Times*—have characterized me as being drunk at this meeting. I don't know where "the paper of record" got this information, but it's completely wrong. I had one drink. A gin and tonic. Whoever leaked this false account also spun that Downer and I met in a random, chance encounter at a trendy bar. But that's false, too. And Downer, who was Australia's foreign minister for many years, obviously has extensive ties to intelligence operatives. So this meeting was anything but random. Intelligence operatives engineered it.

Why would Downer want to meet me, beyond the fact that I had a role advising the Trump campaign? Was it really David Cameron's honor he was protecting? Since Downer has become a player in Russia-Gate, a number of interesting revelations have surfaced.

When Downer told me he was a Hillary Clinton fan, he wasn't kidding. It turns out that, as Australia's foreign minister, he engineered one of the biggest donations to the Clinton Foundation. As *The Hill* reported, he got the Aussie government to pony up $25 million for an AIDS research project administered by the Foundation. When the deal was done—which was part of the Australian government's $2 billion spend on foreign aid in 2006—he posed with Bill Clinton for a handshake. Both men have enormous mutual-admiration-society grins on their faces.

So, Downer had a stake in a Hillary Clinton presidency. He had connections to the former president, and he was undeniably, unabashedly singing her praises to me while bashing Trump. Did that drive his actions? Was he looking to cause harm to the Trump campaign and manufacture an investigation?

In his telling, he was just sharing disturbing information he had stumbled across. Yet, in an April 28, 2018, interview with

The Australian, he admits that nothing I said "indicated Trump himself had been conspiring with the Russians to collect information on Hillary Clinton…He didn't say Trump knew or that Trump was in any way involved in this. He said it was about Russians and Hillary Clinton; it wasn't about Trump."

While that sounds even-handed and fair, let's not kid ourselves. He didn't need me to mention Trump to ignite an investigation. All he needed was someone on the campaign to mention the R-word and repeat a rumor that could be interpreted as calculated election interference. The mere suggestion of impropriety would kick off a full-fledged FBI investigation. And that's exactly what happened.

Looking back at his overheated words and his overt taping of our conversation, it's hard not to think I got played, that he went into the meeting gunning for me, tripping me, and goading me with his Cyprus-baiting, pro-Turkey stance, and his Trump denigration. What was his motive? Had he been tipped off by an intelligence source? I understand that I was part of a controversial campaign and that I was in the line of fire, so to speak, especially after the *Times of London* article. But there were a lot of loose threads out there: A former FBI lawyer at a bizarre London think tank, a meeting at a university used as a CIA training ground, a mysterious professor named Mifsud who worked at that university, a blonde woman play-acting as Putin's niece, a Russian think tank vet named Timofeev, a British reporter with close ties to Downing Street, two diplomats who were probably CIA agents, an Israeli diplomat who introduced me to his girlfriend who was an Australian intelligence officer.

So many threads.

I didn't understand how they fit together. Hell, at that time I didn't even suspect they might be part of the same tapestry.

So, it never occurred to me to ask what the tapestry will reveal when all the threads come together. Or to think of the story it might tell.

Or whose face would be at the center.

Back to 2016: A few days after meeting Downer, I'm invited to a party at the London Hilton. It's part of Israeli Independence Day festivities thrown by the Israeli embassy. I immediately run into Christian Cantor and Erika Thompson. They act as if they are chaperoning me, introducing me to various diplomats including the head of the Middle East division of the US embassy in London. She looks at me with scorn and horror, as if I have some kind of toxic disease.

"Your candidate has no shot in hell of winning the election," she says.

How do you respond to something like that—from a US diplomat, no less?

"Oh, look who's here," Erika says.

It's Alexander Downer.

He walks over to me.

"Nice to see you," I say.

"Hrrmpf," he says as he shakes my hand. He says nothing else. His eyes narrow. Looks have meanings. This one says: I'm watching you.

That's the last time I ever see the man who turns my life into a living hell, igniting a counterintelligence investigation operation.

It's called Operation Crossfire Hurricane. And I'm about to be swept up in it.

CHAPTER 7

GREECE, CLEVELAND & MILLIAN

I T'S THE MIDDLE of May and Trump is steamrolling toward the Republican Party nomination. I am in daily contact with a number of campaign insiders—Stephen Miller, Hope Hicks, Sam Clovis, Steve Bannon. I sense growing confidence within the Trump team. We've all been proven right while the beltway prognosticators and pundits have been proven wrong.

Unfortunately, I slowly discover I've been wrong about something, too: Joseph Mifsud. My attempts at facilitating a meeting between Trump and Russian leadership are going nowhere. As far as opening a portal—a connection to Russian leadership—he's an utter failure. He's succeeded in two things: stirring up hopes and making me look bad. I feel as if I've been played. But I'm not sure what his game is.

At my worst moment, feelings of not making things happen begin to snowball, and I'm concerned that my stature within the policy team is in doubt. I haven't delivered. So I keep in contact with the campaign, but everything is on a low boil. And I stop mentioning Russia at all.

In late May, I head to Athens for a working vacation. I email Sam Clovis and Corey Lewandowski that I'm going to Greece and will let them know how things go. For the campaign work, I have two goals. I want to understand the current US-Greece relationship better, so that, by extension, we can connect with Greek-American voters. I also want to learn about NATO's role in the Mediterranean. Trump has recently flagged Greece as one of only five NATO members spending two percent of its GDP on the organization, and I wondered if this fact could further cement a US-Greece alliance.

Also on my to-do list: visit with relatives. Hang out with my good friend Andreas Papakyriakopoulos, who operates a website called Olympia.gr and runs communications for the Greek government. And see the US attaché in Athens, Robert Palm Jr.—who Terrence Dudley and Gregory Baker from the US embassy in London have requested I meet.

I schedule a meeting with the Greek defense minister, Panos Kammenos, a right-wing politician who is very pro-United States and anti-Islamist, and we agree over the phone to go out for food and drinks at a stylish spot in Kolonaki. When I show up, a member of Kammenos's team greets me.

"You can never be too careful, Mr. Papadopoulos," he says. "Please take the battery out of your phone."

"Of course," I say. Obviously, it's a security measure. I think about the meeting at Trump Hotel; the Secret Service didn't say a damn thing about phones. I wonder if someone recorded that meeting.

When I get to the table to meet Kammenos, he hands his phone to the assistant. I do the same. We sit down and enjoy the view of the Aegean Sea. It is a great dinner. He is a gregarious, funny man, and there is instant chemistry. We drink ouzo, Greece's anise-flavored liqueur, and get a little buzzed. Kammenos expresses his ardent support for Trump and starts ripping into Hillary Clinton, saying, "There's no way in hell we can allow this! It's a disaster."

He also lashes out at Obama. "Papadopoulos," he says. "You need to help me. Obama's shitting on me. He thinks I'm some sort of Russia supporter. I want to be NATO's best friend in the Mediterranean. My objective is to have the United States move its nuclear weapons from Incirlik Air Base in Turkey to Souda Bay, a naval installation on Crete. You need to introduce me to the US ambassador here and the military attaché."

This is exactly the kind of strategic thinking I proposed back when I worked at the Hudson Institute. "I can do that. Absolutely," I say.

"Ash Carter humiliated me when he was defense secretary," he says about Obama's old cabinet member. "He had me meet with his deputy."

"I'm more than happy to talk to Robert Palm, the defense attaché in Athens. That can happen," I say. "But I need a favor from you. I think Trump and Egyptian president Sisi would be a good match. But I haven't developed any connections at the embassy here. I know you guys have an excellent relationship with Egypt. Is there any way that you could hook me up?"

He turns to his assistant. "Go get my phone."

Then he calls the Egyptian defense minister. "You need to meet with Papadopoulos. He needs to meet your people because he's an advisor to Trump."

I'm laughing when he hangs up the phone. That was above and beyond the call of duty.

"Panos," I say. "Can you just introduce me to someone in their embassy here in Athens?"

Now he grabs the phone again and calls a connection at the Greek Ministry of Foreign Affairs. "Get Papadopoulos a meeting with the Egyptian ambassador tomorrow."

We have another glass of ouzo. I toast my good fortune.

The next day I stop by the Greek Ministry of Foreign Affairs. The head of the Middle East division makes a phone call, and I'm invited to go right next door—to the Egyptian embassy.

I walk in and the security guards start talking to me in Arabic. I guess they think I look Egyptian. I answer in English and Greek. Eventually, I meet Ahmed Abu Mussa, the political counselor, and pretty soon I'm having Egyptian coffee, baklava, and cigarettes—even though I don't smoke—with Mussa and the ambassador, Mohamed Farid Monib. It's one of the most friendly, low-key meetings I've ever had. And then they start talking to me about their election concerns.

"Look, George, if Clinton wins, this is going to be really horrible for relations with us. She supported the Muslim Brotherhood; she'll probably freeze weapons to us."

"I'm not here to negotiate. I'm not a US government official," I say. "I'm just here to understand what the US-Egypt relationship is all about. And I hear your concerns. I think solidifying the US-Egypt relationship is important for both sides. Trump and Sisi would get along. Let's talk about setting up a meeting between them in the future."

Call it intuition. Call it the fact that both men were controversial outsiders. But I think a meeting would go well, that they'd have a certain chemistry. I also think Trump needs to show he has some international clout. He caught a lot of flak for immigration plans and statements that were attacked as anti-Muslim. Meeting Sisi, the strongman leader of one of the most prominent Muslim nations in the world, would send a different message.

I also know the United States provides a vast amount of military aid to Egypt, and that Sisi would not want to bite the hand that provided that aid. Fortunately, the ambassador agrees with me.

"I like your style," he says. "Let's stay in contact about this meeting idea."

I am thrilled. Another possible contact is in motion for the campaign. That's my attitude.

I meet with Ahmed Abu Mussa at the Hotel Grande Bretagne a few times during the week to chat and smoke cigars.

OLD WORLD NETWORKING

The Grande Bretagne is a famous hotel right next to Syntagma Square in the center of Athens. Initially built in 1842, it has been a magnet for Greek politicians and foreign powers. During World War II, it served as Athens's Nazi headquarters— until the liberating British forces took their place. During the Greek Civil War, which erupted in 1946, it housed Prime Minister Georgios Papandreou and the Council of Ministers. I end up there again for a meeting with Captain Robert Palm Jr., the defense attaché of the US embassy in Greece.

It's an interesting meeting. Terrence Dudley and Gregory Baker, the two guys from the American embassy in London, have already mentioned Palm to me. Not only that, prior to our get-together, they mistakenly CC'd me on an email.

"He is a subject of interest with many connections in Athens," reads part of the email. "And you need to meet with them."

So I know that Palm has been told to watch me and meet with my connections. For all I know, he's had someone tailing me as

I've been going to meetings. This email makes me wonder who else is watching me. MI6? Did Downer flag me to Australian intelligence? Ditto Christian Cantor and Israel's Mossad or Shin Bet? As for Greece's intelligence agency, why not?

During my meeting with Palm, the subject of the Balkans comes up. And I see this is an excellent way to return the favor of Defense Minister Panos Kammenos, who arranged for me to meet the Egyptians.

"You need to make sure that Russia and China aren't playing around in NATO's backyard," I say. "You really want to keep Russia out of the Balkans as much as possible."

"I didn't realize the Balkans was part of your expertise," Palm says.

I laugh. "It's not really—although my family considers ourselves true Macedonians. But I know some of these guys. You really should meet with Panos Kammenos. The Greeks can be key players to help you. They want to work with the United States."

A few days later, I learn that Palm and the US ambassador meet Panos. Both parties thank me for my intermediary role.

MY BIG MISTAKE

I'm feeling great about my work in Athens. And then on May 26, I screw up.

I have a meeting with the Greek foreign minister, Nikolaos Kotzias. It's an interesting juxtaposition. Kammenos, the defense minister, is from a right-wing background. Kotzias, however, is a former member of the Communist Party of Greece and a Marxist scholar. Greece at this time is ruled by a coalition government, which makes for unexpected alliances.

Right away, Kotzias tells me how important it is for Greece to work with both Russia and the United States, and how Greece can be kind of an intermediary between the two nations.

His tone is very warm, very positive. It's another friendly meeting, with coffee and fruit served.

Then he tells me that tomorrow, Russian leader Vladimir Putin is arriving. "He'll be sitting right where you are sitting."

This information throws me off my game. After all the constant drumbeat of Russia, Russia, Russia that seems to engulf me everywhere I go, I lose my perspective and the diplomatic tone I always want to strike. I say:

"I've heard the Russians have Hillary Clinton's emails."

It is one of those horrible, idiotic moments everyone has. As soon as the words are uttered, you want to reach out and take them back.

But you can't.

The foreign minister's mood changes instantly. His eyes narrow.

"Do not ever repeat that again. That is not something that should ever be mentioned."

I'm in shock. First by his reaction. Then at my own stupidity and the realization that he might actually share with Putin that Americans know about the emails. Would that somehow have an impact on the campaign or me?

I can't believe what I've just done. I guess part of me wanted to impress him by sharing inside information. It was a stupid, stupid thing to do.

He comes over and shakes my hand. It's weird. I was just admonished. Now I get the sense he's trying to comfort me— like that was a moment of discipline, but that we now share a secret that will never be spoken of again.

But how much of a secret do we have? If he's warning me to be silent, can I assume he's going to follow suit? I leave the meeting and head back to my hotel. My head is spinning. Did I just make a huge mistake? Did I totally embarrass myself? What the fuck did I do? I just told a committed Marxist that Russia had Clinton's emails, and he was meeting Putin the next day—and then accompanying him on a pilgrimage to the Holy Mountain of Athos.

Of course, Putin has as much in common with Karl Marx as he does with Groucho Marx, but still.

I'm mad that I've let my guard down. I've behaved like a foolish amateur. It is not a good feeling. I resolve to do better.

Later I hear that Putin wanted to stay at the Grande Bretagne—but his team didn't book rooms in time and nothing was available. If they can't book a hotel room, I think, how can they steal emails? Maybe Mifsud's story is bullshit. Everything else he told me was.

ENTER MILLIAN

I leave Europe in June and relocate to Chicago at my mother's home. I have some savings, but I am very grateful to have my parents' support while I'm volunteering for the campaign. Without it, my work would have been impossible.

I'm getting settled. But I'm also making plans to attend the Republican National Convention. I'm excited to finally meet so many of the people I've been working with.

On July 15—three days before the convention opens—I get an email on LinkedIn:

11:05   .ıl LTE ▭

<   **Sergei Millian**
     • Mobile • 10h ago   •••

JUL 15, 2016

 Sergei Millian • 10:22 am
Dear George, thank you your kind
connection. I would like to remind your
reputable team that I had a pleasure of
exclusively representing Mr Trump's real
estate project Trump Hollywood in Russia
with great success. Besides, I worked as
president of New York-based Russian
American Chamber of Commerce in the USA.
As a result I have insider knowledge and
direct access to the top hierarchy in Russian
politics(president circle, ministers, governors
level). I am an American citizen and a
contributing GOP member. It will be an honor
to provide any type of assistance or advice
needed to you and Mr Trump's team at this
important time in American politics. Please do
not hesitate to contact me at +1 212 ▮▮▮▮▮
▮▮▮▮ or my personal email
▮▮▮▮▮▮▮@▮▮▮.com

Best regards,
Sergei Millian

PS I am currently on business trip to Asia

Write a message...   ⌃

@   ⌾   GIF   ⛓   🎤   Send

After bombing out with Mifsud, I'm a little apprehensive about pursuing another avenue to engineer a meeting with Russians. But then I remember what Clovis said and what Trump himself has repeatedly said: that he's open to dialogue and change with Russians. Now here's another guy offering his services, and he may have ties to help our campaign. I email him back suggesting we connect in the near future. Then I head to Ohio.

IN CONTENTION AT THE CONVENTION

I've been asked to speak on a panel discussion, "Defining America's Role in Global Affairs," on July 20 at the City Club in Cleveland. When I show up, I find out that the other panelists are: US Sen. Bob Corker, R-Tenn., chairman of the Senate Foreign Relations Committee; Congressman Tom Marino, R-Pa., and Ted Yoho, R-Fla., both members of the House Committee on Foreign Affairs; and David O'Sullivan, the EU representative to Washington.

I'm honored to be up there, but more importantly, this is a great opportunity for me to get back in the good graces of the campaign and Trump's policy team. One month earlier, on June 20, campaign manager Corey Lewandowski, my initial contact on the Trump team, was fired. I'd also failed to arrange a meeting with Putin or any Russians. So I'm concerned that my star, such as it is, has fallen. I need a new rabbi.

Marino, in particular, is of interest to me. I know that he is close to the campaign and an outspoken ally of Trump, so I want to leave a positive impression.

Fortunately, as the discussion bounces from multilateral trade agreements to US diplomatic strength and the "Iran deal," I more than hold my own. From my recent meetings in Europe, I know firsthand just how dominant and essential the United States is and how nations look to us for guidance and leadership. So I share that insight. I also get into it with the EU big shot O'Sullivan, and I point out how the European Union was trying to withhold sanctions in the Iran deal because European businesses have money to be made for working with the rogue state.

By the end, Marino pats me on the back and shakes my hand. He's very enthusiastic about my contribution to the discussion. He tells me I should expect a call from Rick Dearborn, Jeff Sessions's former chief of staff, who is now heading the campaign policy team. This is exactly what I want to hear. I am beyond relieved.

A Japanese diplomat, Nagano Masamitsu, from the embassy in D.C. introduces himself to me, along with a colleague from the Ministry of Foreign Affairs. They invite me out for coffee, and one cup of joe turns into a two-hour conversation. This is my first contact with Asian diplomats, and eventually, I connect Nagano with the campaign to arrange liaisons with Japan's golf-loving leader Shinzo Abe, who will become the first foreign leader to meet Trump, just nine days after he wins the November 9 election.

That afternoon, I get an email from Rick Dearborn asking if I can meet with him. I am stoked now. I couldn't have scripted things any better.

I stop by the Hilton, which is Republican Party Celebrity Central. Chris Christie is coming out of the elevator. George Stephanopoulos is on his cell phone. Newt Gingrich walks through the lobby. Corey Lewandowski is there. So is Sam Clovis, who says hi.

I locate Dearborn, who is with another campaign bigwig, John Mashburn.

"So you're the Papadopoulos guy," Dearborn says.

I don't know what that means. I say, "Yeah, I'm George."

"We've been hearing a lot about your foreign travels and what you're doing."

I'm in the dark as to what they think about my work. "I'm just trying to make contacts that can be useful to the campaign," I say.

"We've been hearing what you're trying to put together, and we're very interested."

They tell me they know about my meeting with the Egyptians, which I'd reported back on, and my meeting with the defense minister in Greece. Nobody mentions Russia, which is fine with me since that's the one area in which I haven't delivered. The tone is enthusiastic. Then Dearborn introduces me to Bo Denysyk, national coalition director for the Trump 2016 campaign, who has decades of experience making presidential runs, dating back to Ronald Reagan.

"We want you to lead a 'Greeks for Trump' coalition as well as your duties as a foreign policy advisor," he says. We talk about demographics-focused groups within the campaign who would energize different voter bases. "You should work with George Gigicos," he tells me.

Dearborn comes by again and shakes my hand. "Keep it up," Dearborn says. "Let's be in touch."

"Absolutely," I say.

I'm flying high. I'm back in the thick of the campaign. I hope it's not a fleeting feeling.

A week after the RNC convention, Talia Leibovich, the assistant to the deputy chief of mission at the Israeli embassy, reaches out to me. Oded Joseph, deputy of the Israeli National Security Council's Foreign Policy Division, is coming to Washington. Leibovich asks if I will meet with him to discuss the

Trump campaign. For the first time, I email Dearborn and Michael Glassner, and forward the request. They say, please, we'd like for you to meet him. I meet Joseph in D.C. It's very informal and informational. Joseph wants to cover all the bases and get a read on Trump, and make sure there are no cracks in the relationship.

I send Dearborn an update. From that point forward, Trump's future transition team director and deputy chief of staff is my point of contact.

MEET MR. MILLIAN

A few days later I set up my first meeting with Sergei Millian at the Andaz Hotel right across from the New York Public Library. The Andaz London was where the last guy I talked to about Russia connections—Joseph Mifsud—spilled the Clinton email dirt to me. Now I'm about to meet another guy who claims to have Russian contacts. Coincidence? I have no idea.

Sergei is in his late thirties, which makes him relatively young compared to many of the policy guys and diplomacy people I've been meeting. He's excited to see me. And then, he pulls out a phone and places it in the middle of the table. I don't say anything about the phone, but I do find the placement disturbing. His pitch reiterates some of what he told me in his email. It goes like this:

> I'm a big supporter of candidate Trump. I know Michael Cohen very well. I exclusively represented Mr. Trump's real estate project Trump Hollywood in Russia. I have a lot of connections with Russian business leaders. I want to introduce you to the Russian-American church

here in New York so that you can get the Russian-American community to vote for Trump.

I'm thinking: I just got rid of that loser Mifsud, who introduced me to no one of substance. But this guy Millian sounds like the real deal. He says he knows Trump. He's Belarus-born. He speaks Russian and is the leader of a Russian-American business group.

All of this is very interesting. I realize the campaign is lukewarm about connecting with Russia. But Trump has been talking about Russia for his entire run, and it seems hard to believe—for me, at least—that the campaign would want to shut the door entirely on Russia.

"I can introduce you to a lot of people in Russia," he goes on, with a pitch that echoes Mifsud. "I could be a middleman for you."

He shares more details about what he's done. I say, "Okay, great to meet you. Let's keep in touch."

Within a week of meeting, he emails me with an invitation to an energy conference in Moscow: "It will be my pleasure and honor to arrange energy meetings, extensive briefings from top energy experts in Russia and Europe (including top executives and government decision makers), scheduling your speaking arrangements, and anything else that is within my scope of connections and business experience."

I take a chance and flag the invite to Rick Dearborn. His response is quick and direct. *No. Don't waste your time.*

For me, it is a "message received" moment. Clearly, the campaign is not that interested in making a Putin meeting happen at this point. It makes sense to tone things down in preparation for the national election. Why give Clinton any more ammunition?

I tell Millian thanks but no thanks. We stay in touch. Sergei is a funny, loose guy. In mid-August of 2016, he meets me in Astoria, Queens, the Greek neighborhood of New York City. We go out to dinner, we talk about the Trump campaign, about politics, about the world, and about Russia, which I tell him not to waste time on. Then he says, "Let's go for a drive."

At one point, we come to a bridge that connects Queens to Roosevelt Island, a small strip of land in the East River that runs parallel to Manhattan. He stops the car. "Go stand over there," he says. "I'll take your picture."

I'm a little surprised. Nobody in my entire professional career has ever asked to take my photo. Just a few months earlier, Alexander Downer took my picture. Now this guy is a shutterbug all of sudden? What the hell? It's weird.

But I don't want to be a drag. I'm thinking, maybe this guy has Instagram fever or something. It's a social media world we live in, after all.

The next time we meet later that month, it's at the basement bar of the Andaz Hotel. The place is deserted when we show up. It's just us and the waitress—as quiet as a morgue, initially. Then a couple comes in and takes the table right next to us.

In a totally empty bar.

At that point, Millian starts talking to me about how he wants to introduce me to Russian officials. Again.

"Sergei," I say, noticing the couple seems to be eavesdropping on us. "I told you, the campaign isn't interested. I'm not going to ask them again about this."

The couple isn't talking. It's hard not to wonder if Sergei and I are targets of some operation. I don't see Sergei for a while after that.

RUSSIA REDUX

Unlike the campaign, the rest of the world is still interested in Russia. In September, around the time Trump and Sisi meet at the UN General Assembly, Tobias Ellwood of the British Foreign Ministry invites me to have a drink in New York. It's a game of 20 Questions with this guy—all about Russia.

> *What are you planning on doing with Russia?*
> *Why does Trump want to work with them?*
> *Why are you promoting this agenda? It's very dangerous.*
> *Don't you realize it's important for Trump to isolate Russia?*
>   *We need the United States to come with the United Kingdom*
>   *to Poland and build bases there and keep Russia out.*

I have to admit, as someone who was born as the Cold War wound down, some of this thinking strikes me as paranoid. As if Moscow is this evil empire with no redeeming qualities. I realize the government's civil rights record is horrible and Putin's affection for the GRU is inescapable. But both nations share concerns about the rise of radical Islam, terrorism, and China's swelling global influence. There should, theoretically, be ways to work together. I report Ellwood's concerns back to Dearborn.

Right after this meeting, Interfax, Russia's leading news agency, contacts Bryan Lanza and Hope Hicks, who were running Trump's policy surrogates. I'm told that Interfax wants to interview me. My instructions are to talk about sanctions and the US-Russia relations in Syria.

Ksenia Baygarova, the reporter, interviews me at the Hilton in Midtown New York. It's the only interview that anyone from the campaign gives to the Russian media.

Two-plus years later, I think this interview holds up very well. It is a very accurate, even-handed appraisal of the state of things. I'm sure cold warriors and social rights activists wish I had lashed out harder at the Putin-ocracy. But I state a number of unassailable facts: That relations between the United States and Russia are extremely tense. That we do have some common goals. That our sanctions against Russia, while hurting Moscow, also serve to benefit China, which is not an ideal situation. The feedback from Trump Tower? Well done.

CHAPTER 8

THE HALPER SET-UP

O N SEPTEMBER 2, 2016, a Cambridge University professor named Stefan Halper emails me out of the blue and invites me to London to discuss the Leviathan natural gas field.

He claims to be leading a project on the Turkey–European Union relationship and how the gas fields in Israel and Cyprus play into that. He notes that I'm a recognized expert in this field and offers to pay me $3,000 and fly me to London for discussions.

If you look up Stefan Halper on Google now, the Wikipedia entry summarizes his career this way: "Stefan A. Halper is an American foreign policy scholar and Senior Fellow at the University of Cambridge where he is a Life Fellow at Magdalene College and directs the Department of Politics and International Studies." That sounds very respectable and responsible.

Dig a little deeper—to the full Wikipedia entry or any number of articles—and you find that this man is anything but a squeaky-clean, policy-wonk academic. Pulitzer Prize-winning journalist Glenn Greenwald—an avowed fan of Edward Snowden and WikiLeaks, it should be noted—has reported that Halper, working within the Reagan administration, managed CIA operatives who spied on President Jimmy Carter's foreign policy team "to ensure the Reagan campaign knew of any foreign policy decisions that Carter was considering." It's worth noting that Reagan's vice president was George H.W. Bush, the former director of the CIA, and Halper is said to have strong ties to the Bush family.

Halper's spy ties don't end there. His father-in-law, Ray Cline, was a top CIA official during the Cold War. Recently, Halper has reportedly worked with MI6, Britain's version of the CIA. Articles in the *Washington Post* and the *Daily Caller* claim that Halper has worked closely with Richard Dearlove, the former chief of MI6, while at Cambridge, directing the Cambridge Security Initiative, an intelligence consulting group that has had UK and US government agencies as clients.

I don't know any of this about Halper when I get his invite. I Google him, but all I see is that he's been in the Ford and Reagan administrations. I don't notice any CIA mentions. So as far as I can see, this is a pretty good deal: I get three grand, a ticket to London, and a five-star hotel; and a legitimate academic gets to pick my brain on the Mediterranean oil world. Hell, it's almost a paid vacation. My girlfriend Salma, who lives in London, and I are in that weird long-distance, what-are-we-doing zone. I can see her at least one more time and figure things out. As far as I'm concerned, the trip is nothing but a win, win, win.

On September 15, I fly to London. I check into the Connaught Hotel, and Halper's research assistant, Azra Turk, messages me. "Let's meet for a drink. I'm looking forward to meeting you."

Is that a suggestive text? I'm not sure. When I arrive at the bar Azra has picked, I change my opinion.

It was definitely suggestive.

Azra Turk is a vision right out of central casting for a spy flick. She's a sexy bottle blonde in her thirties, and she isn't shy about showing her curves—as if anyone could miss them. She's a fantasy's fantasy. "If this is what academic researchers look like, I've been going to the wrong school," I laugh to myself.

We sit down. Azra tells me that she's from a wealthy Turkish family that relocated to Los Angeles, but that she's been working as Halper's research assistant. It takes her about five minutes before she starts asking me about the Trump campaign. She wants to know: are we working with Russia?

"I don't know what you are talking about," I say with a nervous laugh—her question is creepy. "I have nothing to do with Russia, and I don't know anyone else who has anything to do with Russia, either."

But she keeps pushing. She puts her hand on my arm. She says I'm more attractive in person than in my pictures. She says I've been doing important work. It's all a come-on. Still, I want to believe she's a research assistant because if she isn't, this woman is an operative of some kind. "I'd love to hear more about the campaign. It is such a fascinating subject. How is Trump going to win? How can he beat Hillary Clinton?"

I've shot her down on Russia, but she's still asking me for campaign tactics.

"I didn't come here to talk about the campaign. I thought you guys wanted to hear about the Leviathan gas field."

Now she laughs. The flirting continues. She asks me personal questions.

I am astonished. This is supposed to be a business meeting. I can't believe how unprofessional she is. I'm thinking, "There is no way this is a Cambridge professor's research assistant. The only thing she seems to want to research is Trump, Russia, and me."

We get to the end of our drinks, and I say goodbye. I return to my room and describe the meeting to Salma. I'm stunned by the come-hither tone of Azra Turk and her classic honey-pot act.

Salma laughs. I'm not sure she believes me. Who can blame her? I'm not a Don Juan or secret agent. I'm a policy guy. Azra Turk was acting like I was James Bond. It didn't make any sense.

THE WALRUS

Stefan Halper is a morbidly obese seventy-three-year-old American. His girth has earned him an unflattering nickname in the intelligence community: The Walrus. We meet for the first time at the Traveler's Club, another of London's Old-World institutions. Located in tony Pall Mall, the club's elegant 1832 building was inspired by Raphael's Palazzo Pandolfini in Florence. I walk in, dwarfed by the high ceilings, and can see why ambassadors and high commissioners and other senior diplomats frequent the club. It's genteel—the last place you'd go expecting a hostile interrogation.

I go upstairs and find The Walrus sitting in a private room. He is cartoonishly massive, and the cartoonishly voluptuous Azra Turk is with him. Once again, her provocative outfit defies expectations. But with Halper in the room, her behavior is much more demure than the previous evening. She gets us coffee. I wonder what their relationship is since she really doesn't come across as an academic.

Halper is sweating from the moment I walk in. He also seems to be channeling Alexander Downer. Like Downer, he immediately launches into a foul-mouthed rant. He's talking to me about Cyprus, Turkey, and energy—just like Alexander Downer had—except, he homes in even more about Turkey, making it clear he's very hostile to my stance on the future of Mediterranean energy alliances. This is how I remember the exchange.

"You are wrong," he says. "Everything you say about Turkey is wrong. They are our ally. Your positions on the whole area are against US intelligence assessments."

"How am I wrong on Erdoğan?" I ask. "Did I miss something? Has Erdoğan renounced Islamic law?"

"He is an ally. You need to rethink your entire understanding of the Mediterranean."

"I think I understand it pretty well."

"No, you fucking don't."

"Erdoğan is power-crazed and an Islamist."

"He's a great ally—and a buffer between the Iranians, the Saudis, ISIS, and Russia."

"Right. Because he wants to be more powerful than those regimes."

"You don't know what you're talking about. This is the fucking real world. Turkey is too important to alienate."

This is incredible. This guy didn't fly me here and pay me to share my expertise on energy issues. He brought me here to lecture me and tell me that I'm entirely wrong about Turkey. I don't get it.

"Are you pushing this idiocy on Trump?"

"Excuse me?"

"Is the campaign interested in your ideas?"

"You'll have to ask Mr. Trump."

Now this exchange starts to make a little more sense to me.

The guys from the US embassies in London and Athens were very nervous about what I was recommending about Turkey. Downer, too, mentioned this stuff. Everyone wants to find out if I'm advising Trump on Greece, Cyprus, Israel, Turkey, Egypt, and the Leviathan gas field. Halper continues the trend—but his tactics need work. He's just attacking me, like some bully.

After more mini-lectures—on Turkey's then-booming economy (by June of 2018, the nation's over-extended economy was teetering on the precipice of collapse), on the importance of its proximity to Russia, on how Israel needs strong relations with Turkey just as much as it does with Egypt, and on how military bases on Greek islands won't necessarily provide a strong military buffer to Turkey or Russia—I'm tired and annoyed. Nobody likes getting badgered. It's insulting.

The Walrus also continues sweating profusely, which is disturbing considering we are just talking. I wonder if he's going to have a heart attack.

"I didn't fly here to argue with you," I say. "You said you wanted my insight and opinions on this sphere. If that's not the case, let me know."

"I still do. Please write them up. Fifteen hundred words."

As I leave Halper to enjoy the company of his assistant, I get an email from the British Ministry of Foreign Affairs. They would like to meet with me. Could I come by the Foreign Commonwealth Office and see Tobias Ellwood?

This is pretty interesting. How do they know I am even in town? I suppose it could be a total coincidence. Or perhaps Halper told someone.

Or someone could be spying on me.

But thinking like that is a sign of paranoia and negativity.

I don't want to be paranoid or negative.

So I laugh off the thought and arrange to meet Ellwood.

MORE TRUMP JITTERS

Tobias Ellwood, a member of Parliament and Junior Foreign Minister, is the negative image of Halper: comparatively youthful, gracious, polite. He and another colleague thank me for taking the time to meet.

Like Halper, they seem to have a message to deliver. They tell me that Brexit is a disaster for England and that Trump's support for Brexit isn't helping things. "He doesn't know what he's talking about," Ellwood tells me. "It's lamentable your country has supported such a disastrous candidate. And that he's urging our exit."

As nice as these guys are, I am stunned. Ellwood is a Conservative Party bigwig. The Conservatives supported Brexit! Now here's a guy telling me the departure from the European Union is a nightmare that will ultimately hurt England. Then they ask me for various insights on Trump's views on the relationship with the United Kingdom moving forward, as well as his views on Iran and Russia. My responses echo the previous lines of Trump's campaign. But I assure them that he is not at all hostile to the United Kingdom, where he even has golf courses. As a businessman, he is very aware of the world's fifth largest economy.

HALPER HELL

Worst. London. Trip. Ever. That's what I think when I get out of the Foreign Office. I'm three-for-three: every meeting I've had—from Azra Turk's sultry come-ons to the Halper lecture series to this Foreign Office shake-down—has been a waste of time. I'm actually looking forward to leaving the next day to go back to Chicago.

Then Halper calls again.

Just the guy to brighten my mood.

"I want you to meet me at the Sofitel for a goodbye drink."

He's a jerk. But he's a paying customer. I agree.

The next day, I show up at the hotel. The Walrus is there. Without Azra this time.

We order gin and tonics. He pulls his phone out and puts it on the table. Yes, I realize many people like to keep their phone handy—despite the fact that it's a rude thing to do. But he doesn't place the phone near him to keep an eye out on incoming messages. He pushed it toward me. Just like Downer.

Why is this guy recording me? I have no idea, but l don't say anything about it. I have nothing to hide.

Halper immediately launches into a series of leading questions.

It's great that Russia is helping you and the campaign, right, George?

George, you and your campaign are involved in hacking and working with Russia, right?

It seems like you are a middleman for Trump and Russia, right?

I know you know about the emails.

He's basically making outrageous, bogus statements and asking me to confirm them. Remember, by this time, the entire world knows Russia's GRU operatives have hacked the Democratic National Committee. The DNC had confirmed the hack back in June, and emails have been published steadily on WikiLeaks. So these suggestions—about my being involved in some kind of conspiracy—are not just absolutely outrageous and false, they are dangerous.

"I don't know what the fuck you're talking about," I say. I rarely curse in a professional setting, but that's how angry I am. This is the second time in three days that someone has mentioned conspiring with Russia—Halper's honeypot assistant tried to do the same thing. "This is bullshit," I say.

"I'm talking about the Russians and Trump," says Halper.

"Well, I have no idea what the hell you are talking about. What you are talking about is treason. And I have nothing to do with Russia, so stop bothering me about it."

The Walrus is sweating again. The fat bastard's face is tight with anger. He takes his phone back and puts in his pocket. I stand up.

"I'll be turning in my report next week," I say. I get the hell out of there. I send him my report. But I never hear from him again.

LET MY PEOPLE KNOW

While Halper and the British Foreign Office are playing head games with me, I'm also trying to do some work for the campaign. My contacts in Egypt have reached out to me. Egyptian president Abdel Fattah al-Sisi is going to New York to address the UN General Assembly. He is interested in meeting Trump.

I email Steve Bannon to let him know that I'm in London but that Sisi wants to meet Trump, and he should really make this happen. Bannon calls me, and I introduce him to Yasser El-Shemy, my old contact at the Egyptian embassy in D.C. As I understand it, Bannon talks with El-Shemy and Egyptian ambassador Yasser Reda, and the powwow is set in motion. Trump and Sisi are going to get together.

The meeting generates big headlines. It's the first time candidate Trump has met with a foreign leader. Hillary Clinton also meets with Sisi. So Trump looks just as much a seasoned leader as the former secretary of state. I'm in Greece when the tête-à-tête takes place. But I can see from 4000 miles away that it generates good optics.

So much for my being a coffee boy.

FLASHING FORWARD AND BACK

As of this writing, I've found out many interesting things about Stefan Halper, Alexander Downer, and some of Trump's foreign policy advisors.

I learn that Halper is also connected to Hakluyt—the same intelligence shop that Downer, claiming he was a board member, bragged to me about. I also discover, via an excellent piece by John Solomon in *The Hill,* that "according to documents and government interviews, one of the FBI's most senior counterintelligence agents visited London the first week of May 2016." One week later, on May 10, I met Alexander Downer, who discussed many of the same topics that Halper later brought up.

Solomon's article also reports that in June 2016 a Cambridge University graduate student who studied with Halper invited Carter Page, the so-called Russia expert on Trump's advisory panel, to a London security conference.

There, Page met with Halper, and the two remained in contact. Halper eventually asked to be introduced to Sam Clovis, and Page obliged, sending a suck-up email: "Professor Stef Halper spends part of the year in Virginia where he has a home in Falls Church; he's a big fan of yours, having followed you on CNN, and offered a range of possibilities about how he and the university might be able to help."

When that entreaty failed, Halper approached Clovis himself with a late-August email, telling him he'd been in contact with Page, and that Page suggested the two men talk. A few days later, they met. According to Clovis, Halper pitched himself as a China expert—slightly different than the Mediterranean wizard he pretended to be with me. What was Halper's game? Clovis, in an interview with the *Washington Examiner*, says the whole point was to get me: "I think [Halper] was using his meeting with me to give him bona fides to talk to George Papadopoulos. He used Carter Page to get to me and he used me to get to George. George was the target. I think George was the target all along."

I agree. But the question is why? What was Halper's mission in getting to me? It has now been widely reported that Halper was working as an informant for the FBI. In fact, the Bureau and members of Congress bent over backward trying to shield Halper's identity after news broke in May of 2018 that an FBI informant had been harvesting information on campaign members. So he was working for the FBI. What was their game?

When I replay my Halper meeting in my head, it is striking how similar it was to my encounter with Downer, how the subject matter was the same. Downer opened with a remark about me bothering Cameron, but he then immediately launched into Turkey, Greece, and Cyprus. He had also told me he knew all about me. Halper had done the same things. It seemed like his mission was to duplicate the Downer meeting and extract more damning specifics.

Let's assume Downer and I talked about Russia meddling in the election. I don't remember doing that, but let's say I did mention something. Maybe it was just "the Russians have a surprise for Clinton." That's not enough to tie me or, more importantly, Trump and the campaign to any sinister collusion allegations. Somebody wanted more.

There's another reason to draft Halper into the sting operation. If he succeeded in getting me to admit anything about Russia and the campaign or Hillary Clinton's emails, then Downer's flimsy allegation wouldn't even be needed. The storyline of the investigation would have given all the glory to the FBI and maybe some Cambridge professor with ties to the CIA and Ronald Reagan. Downer has strong connections to the Clintons, which might make his version of events suspect. By using Halper as an informant, Downer, the primary source to kick off the whole "collusion conspiracy," wouldn't be needed. The man who evidently worked with intelligence agencies—God only knows which ones—to manufacture evidence against me and drive the entire Trump-Russia narrative forward would be invisible.

I'm sure some people will dismiss this idea—cue the refrain that I'm naive or delusional or too young to know what I'm talking about. Bear with me: I respect our law enforcement and intelligence services. I believe that 99% of the people that work for the Department of Justice, the FBI, and the CIA are brave, decent people out to uphold the law, protect American interests, and do the right thing. That said, both the FBI and the CIA have long, tainted histories. These are not infallible organizations. Under J. Edgar Hoover, the FBI spied on thousands of innocent Americans, violating their constitutional right to privacy because of suspicions about their political beliefs, their religious beliefs, sexual preferences, and more. The CIA? It has spied on Americans, too. And it has repeatedly been connected to plots to assassinate foreign leaders of Congo, Cuba, Nicaragua, South Vietnam, and other nations. The spy agency—under the direction of President Richard Nixon—also engineered the coup d'état against democratically elected Chilean president Salvador Allende, which ended in Allende's death, supposedly by "suicide." In other words, the honor code of the CIA and FBI can and has completely vanished when truth, democracy, and civil rights are deemed inconvenient to furthering American interests.

No doubt, a fair national election is in the American interest. Any interference in this process should be viewed as a hostile act, if not an outright act of war. So I get investigating the Clinton emails leak. I get investigating Donald Trump Jr. for holding a meeting with Russians and telling them he'd love damaging information on Clinton—although, really, who wouldn't? I understand that Trump thanking WikiLeaks and appealing to them to find Clinton's missing emails was dangerous and unpresidential—especially since WikiLeaks has been so hostile to US interests in the past.

But I don't get planting information on an unsuspecting, young campaign advisor and then trying to manufacture a vast conspiracy. At best, it's prosecutorial overreach; at worst, it's the deep state declaring war on Donald Trump—and with that, a war on truth, justice, and the American way.

THE DEEP STATE

The deep state is not a place. It doesn't issue passports. You can't go there for a visit.

The deep state isn't an official organization, either. There's no charter. It has no rules of order.

But it does have rules of disorder.

In fact, that may be its primary mission: to sow chaos within America and wage a covert war against the president of the United States and the Republican Party.

The deep state is the movement of anti-Trump operatives in America's three branches of government who have been working against Donald Trump, his campaign, and his administration to strip it of authority.

These operatives are government employees loyal to Hillary Clinton and Barack Obama. They are hellbent on playing politics and using the tools of the state—politically driven investigations, rubber-stamped FISA warrants, leaked memos and legal documents—as well as planted stories in the press and social media to wage war on Trump, his team, and the Republican Party.

For much of the mainstream media, the idea of a deep state is derided as a conservative conspiracy theory, a last-resort defense for wrongdoers.

But when the government targets one person after another for political reasons, a conspiracy morphs into a reality. The list of casualties—or should I say victims—is long and growing. I'm just one in a crowd. General Michael Flynn, a life-long patriot, has been drawn and quartered over his failure to adhere to the Foreign Agents Registration Act (FARA). But the fact is that law has been ignored by the DOJ for years, until Trump began his run. As Ken Silverstein wrote for *Politico*, "The law was enacted in 1938, but it's been under-enforced or not enforced at all for ages." I was threatened with the same violation. And it's a safe bet that a number of others on Team Trump were as well. Meanwhile, Carter Page's name has been dragged through the mud for two years—with no charges against him.

Adam Lovinger, a Pentagon analyst who raised questions

about a defense contract given to none other than Stefan Halper, is another victim of the deep state. After Lovinger was appointed to Trump's National Security Council, authorities revoked his security clearance over claims he was seen reading top-secret documents during an airplane ride.

"Security clearances are being weaponized against the White House by hostile career bureaucrats, thwarting the president's agenda by holding up or blocking appointees," according to Lovinger's lawyer, Sean Bigley.

Jobs have been lost, careers destroyed, prison sentences handed out, and millions of dollars wasted as the deep state pursues manufactured or completely overblown violations meant to intimidate and turn evidence on others. Investigations should not be used as tools to terrorize patriots because the powers that be don't like you.

Unfortunately for me, in early October 2016 the powers that be weren't done yet.

ANOTHER SETUP

On October 7, 2016, the *Washington Post* publishes a story—and runs the actual clip on its website—about Donald Trump uttering what is destined to be the most infamous sentence ever unleashed by a future US president: "Grab them by the pussy." I was horrified by this. These were the words of an immature businessman engaged in stupid macho behavior, not the words of someone trying to become the leader of the free world. Honestly, I thought it was a fatal sound bite that would lose Trump the election.

So when Sergei Millian calls me up for a meeting in Chicago to discuss a business proposal, I'm all ears. If Trump loses the election, I have no chance of landing a policy job in D.C. I need a backup plan.

We meet at the Trump Hotel & Tower Chicago on October 15. Sergei launches into his proposal. He is all business. The laughing, joking Sergei—the guy who is always telling me about problems with his Chinese girlfriend whose father is a high-ranking military man in Beijing—is missing. Instead this Sergei Millian is pacing around. He says he wants to pay me $30,000 a month to work as a PR consultant, funded by a former Russian energy minister he never identifies. *I never see a contract.* As far as I am concerned there has never been a real, concrete proposal, so when he came to visit, I was already weary of this flimsy pitch. I listen to plans about a beautiful office in New York. Then I notice something. He's wearing a silk scarf around his neck. Indoors. What does he need a scarf for? He's not some hipster artist. He's a conservative business guy. Is he wearing a wire? I can't believe it. But I think he is. I'm on my guard not to say a damn thing that could be taken the wrong way.

And like Halper, he's visibly sweating. It's freezing outside in Chicago, but he's overheating. "Come over here, George," he motions to me.

I get up and join his parade around the lounge at Trump Tower. I see a group of four men watching us. Are they agents? Who knows?

"George," Sergei says, "You have to understand that it's very common in Russia for people to do business and work for the government at the same time."

I am staggered, insulted, and pissed off—all at the same time. But Sergei isn't finished yet.

"In order for me to pay you $30,000 a month, you have to also work for Trump."

"I don't know what the hell you're talking about, Sergei. That's completely illegal, and I will never accept it. I already made it clear to you even before you came to Chicago that I had certain conditions and that I'd recuse myself from anything related to Trump."

Millian does not like this response. But I don't give a damn. I don't like the offer. It is completely demeaning. It sounds like a bribe, basically.

He is surly and distant. I try to keep things positive. "If you can come up with an agreement where you meet my conditions, let's do it." We finish our martinis, and I confirm plans to go out later for dinner.

"No," he says. "I'm feeling sick. I'm going to leave for New York tonight."

So Millian flew into Chicago and left the same day after making a bizarre offer designed to compromise me while wearing a mysterious scarf around his neck. Three weeks before the election. I'm on my guard with him from now on.

But I'm a little too late. On November 5, just days before the election, Millian forwards me an email he has sent to Hope Hicks in response to an article in the *Financial Times*. He closes his email with something that I find super-creepy in retrospect:

Sergio Millian <████████@██.com>

To: George Papadopoulos <████████, ██@██.com>

Date: Sat, Nov 5, 2016 at 5:56 AM

George,

I just wanted you to know that I wrote this for Mr. Trump. I have no doubt that forces that invested so much into H will try to steal the elections. Otherwise, all the money they paid will go to waste.

Please be very cautious these last few days. Even to the point of not leaving your food and drinks out of eye sight. I saw you in my dream with two men in black with angry faces hiding behind your back.

Best wishes from Zurich!
Sergei

Two men in black?

Was he trying to warn me? Does he know something I don't know? Is he motivated by guilt?

I have no idea. But it does feel like there's a great deal going on behind my back.

THE STEELE FACTOR

Speaking of men in black and cloak-and-dagger intrigue, on October 31, 2016, news breaks about a top-secret dossier with damning allegations about Trump. Reporter David Corn of the liberal publication *Mother Jones* reports that "a former senior intelligence officer for a Western country who specialized in Russian counterintelligence" provided the FBI with memos asserting that Trump had covert relationships with Russia. According to one dispatch viewed by Corn, "Russian regime has been cultivating, supporting and assisting Trump for at least 5 years. Aim, endorsed by Putin, has been to encourage splits and divisions in Western alliance." The memo also noted that Trump "and his inner circle have accepted a regular flow of intelligence from the Kremlin, including on his Democratic and other political rivals."

These are bombshell allegations. Trump, of course, has repeatedly said, "I have nothing to do with Russia." But now a storyline of collusion—something I've been asked about again and again—is developing, and it appears the FBI is investigating.

There are ominous clouds looming over the Trump campaign. I wonder what else the dossier says. And who is behind it.

These questions are answered—or at least some of them—two months later, on January 10, when the website Buzzfeed publishes the full document that Corn cited. It is dubbed the Steele Dossier, named after Christopher Steele, the former head of MI6's Russia desk, who was initially hired by anti-Trump forces to investigate the candidate. This fact immediately calls into question the veracity of the report—was it weaponized to attack Trump? Also straining credulity are many of the dossier's most shocking claims, including a salacious story that suggests Trump was videotaped in a compromising position that could be used as leverage against him by Russia.

Less than two weeks before the election, things are looking quite grim for Team Trump.

CHAPTER 9

VICTORY SPOILS

T HE WORLD CHANGES on November 9, 2016.
Trump scores a monumental upset election victory on that day. Weeks earlier, this just didn't seem possible. Trump was up against negative numbers at the polls, not to mention his sordid comments about women and the vague charges in the mysterious Steele Dossier. But having a tone-deaf, reviled opponent in Hillary Clinton helps. And so does having FBI director James Comey throw an accidental wrench into the election to help Trump achieve the impossible.

Eleven days before the election, Comey sends a letter to Congress announcing he will reopen the Hillary Clinton email investigation to examine new evidence. Comey later claims he thought he would lose his job if he didn't tell Congress about the new development—the discovery of a laptop in possession of Clinton's deputy advisor Huma Abedin that was used by Anthony Weiner, her husband. There is speculation that the computer may contain missing emails. The laptop eventually proves to be another dead end that yields no new evidence against Clinton, but the temporary jumpstart of the investigation reopens Clinton's old wounds with voters.

The rest is, as they say, history.

Or it should have been.

As it turns out, for many people, Trump's unexpected victory amplifies the question of Russian interference in the election. Pundits and nearly sixty-eight million Hillary Clinton voters ask how this upset could have happened. How were the polls so off-base? Something must have gone wrong.

One semi-logical conclusion—given the specter of the Steele Dossier alleging all kinds of sinister charges about Russia and Trump—is that there must have been outside interference. Russian active measures. And worse, given campaign chairman Paul Manafort's strong Russian ties—and the candidate's many overtures to Putin—there must have been collusion between the Trump team and Russia.

So instead of the rest being history, the rest, as my story shows, is unrest. People—intelligence operatives, FBI agents, and Department of Justice investigators—keep trying to rewrite history with investigations, secret operations, active measures, and court filings. And while I do believe that most of these lawmen seek to uncover the truth, their methods of proving collusion, at least where I stand, relied on sting operations that became self-fulfilling prophecies.

But I'm getting a little ahead of myself again.

My phone and email are in overdrive on November 10. Many of my contacts made over the last year reach out to me. I get congratulatory calls from the Greek prime minister and defense minister, as well as from my Egyptian, Japanese, and

Cypriot contacts. They are all eager to work with the new administration.

I get messages from the British Foreign Office, too. Tobias Ellwood says he is sending me Theresa May's letter congratulating Trump. I'm also asked if I can set up a call between the two leaders. When the letter arrives, I pass it along to Steve Bannon. May and Trump eventually speak; I'm not sure if my relaying the messages had anything to do with it, but I'm still feeling pretty damn good about my contributions to the campaign. I hope others feel the same way. It's hard to know, exactly, but my goal of landing a job in the new administration now seems entirely within reach.

I just have to be patient and stay out of trouble.

THE LAST RODEO

About a month after the election, I'm introduced to a man named Father Alex Karloutsos, the head of Department of Public Affairs of the Greek Orthodox Archdiocese of America. He is one of the most politically connected people I have ever met. He knows everyone. He's tight with the Clintons and is a close friend of Joe Biden. He lives in Southampton, the ritzy beach town bastion of New York's liberal elite. But Father Alex, as everyone calls him, has both sides of the political aisle covered. He meets with Mike Pence to discuss religious matters and has been a mentor of sorts to Reince Priebus. In the brief time I spend with him in New York, he introduces me to conservative congressman Ed Royce (R-CA) and billionaire John Catsimatidis, who owns the Gristedes supermarket chain and ran for mayor of New York in 2013. I become a frequent guest in Southampton during my time on the campaign and attend

Saturday breakfast there with a group of New York's business and political elite.

Father Alex's message to me is: "I'm going to get you together with Reince Priebus. It will help you get a job with the administration."

"That would be great."

"But I need you to come to Greece. I'm hosting a conference in Drama." The idea is that he would introduce me as Trump's advisor, which would make him look good.

I don't quite understand this. Father Alex is already close with Priebus. They've worked together for a number of years. He could score plenty of points dropping the name of Trump's future chief of staff. Clearly, though, Reince is too busy with the transition team and controlling access to the president to make the trip. So I guess Father Alex still wanted someone on site with ties to the administration that he could point to: Me.

I fly to Greece with Father Alex. During the trip I meet a number of people who have a misguided idea that my role as a foreign policy advisor somehow means I want to discuss the Trump real estate empire. They ask me to convince the president-elect to build a Trump Hotel in Athens.

I just laugh. "I don't have anything to do with Trump's family business operations."

One guy is very persistent. He wines and dines me. He continues talking to me about Trump and business development plans—despite my admonishments. He has a one-track mind. It is amazing how some people can just ignore what they are being told. As if repeating a question or suggestion will magically change the reality.

This trip is a total waste of time. Fortunately, I have a meeting scheduled with the president of the Cyprus Parliament, Demetris Syllouris. I fly into Nicosia on December 15. My goal is to meet with Cypriot officials to talk about ExxonMobil and other energy businesses getting into the game. And of course, to figure out how to help American interests in the region.

Syllouris takes me to an event tied to Jordan's opening of its first-ever embassy in Cyprus. I meet the Jordanian deputy prime minister and minister of foreign affairs, Nasser Judeh. He's a stocky, short, mustachioed guy. Accompanied by a body-guard, we go to a private room where he dismisses the guard and we begin to discuss US-Jordanian relations.

"Mr. Papadopoulos, I'm in touch with Michael Flynn. We're looking forward to working with you."

But it was clear he was very nervous—like so many other leaders—about what the future held for his nation's relation-ship with the United States under Trump. I send back news of the meeting to Mike Flynn in D.C. He replies, saying he looks forward to meeting me soon.

The next morning, I go to the law office of Nicos Anastasiades, the president of Cyprus, in Limassol, on the southern coast. I haven't seen him since 2014 when I came to the island with Seth Cropsey of the Hudson Institute, but I am honored that he wants to meet and discuss avenues of collaboration between the United States and Cyprus. He's puffing away at a cigar, and he's pretty amped.

"Thank God Trump won! We're looking to do business with America, and Clinton just didn't understand anything, and we hope to attract American investments," he tells me. He waxes on about energy projects, and I float the idea about getting rid of the British bases on Cyprus and replacing them with Ameri-can boots. The Cypriots view the British presence there as a vestige of the vanished English empire. As we talk, an idea crys-talizes in my head: This is another reason why the British, Stefan Halper, and Alexander Downer have zeroed in on me—my connections to Cyprus are at the highest level. The last thing they want is my discussing British troop withdrawal with the president of Cyprus! I had had a similar exchange with the Greek defense minister, where I floated ideas about America building a new base on the island of Karpathos and forging an agreement to vanquish debts in exchange for obtaining all of Greece's natural reserves for American companies.

Both Cypriot and Greek leadership were open to these discussions. In fact, ExxonMobil now has the largest stake in the energy reserves south of the Greek island of Crete, which makes American presence in the area even more logical. Both the company and government are expecting a bonanza. I told President Anastasiades I would pass along his statements to Michael Flynn and Steve Bannon.

And that's precisely what I do. My interactions with the transition team in D.C. are focused entirely on relaying ideas about energy projects in Cyprus and Greece, and how the Greek government is eager to have the United States build a new base on the island of Karpathos, and come to an agreement on debt issues. These were ambitious ideas that they wanted to explore further.

I email Flynn and others. The response is enthusiastic. But, of course, every new administration has to prioritize things, and I have no way of knowing how these proposals get ranked.

I return to the States to play my waiting game.

INAUGURATION AGGRAVATION

Donald Trump's presidential inauguration happens on January 20, 2017. Trump may have a new job, but I am still on the outside looking in. As I set off to Washington for the festivities,

I'm flummoxed about not landing an official position with the administration. I feel like I've acquitted myself quite well as a surrogate for the campaign. I've given interviews that accurately reflect Trump's perspective; helped arrange meetings and contacts; delivered messages. But for some reason, it's not enough. Or I haven't scored points with the right person. I don't get it. But I'm told I will have an interview, finally, just days later. So I still feel like I'm in the game.

That weekend Sergei Millian reaches out to me. He wants to congratulate me on Trump's victory and have a drink. I am still guarded about his shady offer two months earlier in Chicago, but he's kept in touch via email. He's one of those guys who doesn't take no for an answer.

We meet at Russia House, a bustling three-story pierogi and caviar joint near Dupont Circle. In hindsight, it seems like an ironic place to meet. But Sergei chose it. He has a third-wheel with him, a barrel-chested, good-time Charlie in his fifties.

The new guy mentions he used to be married to the daughter of some political bigwig in Georgia. He spends most of his time talking about women. You know: "Wow, check her out!" and, "I get all these chicks," kind of stuff—very juvenile behavior. I remember thinking, what is Sergei doing with this guy? Why am I here with this person? I guess they know each other in Atlanta.

Sergei informs me that he just met with John McCain. When I ask why, he doesn't offer many details. Just that his pal and another friend, Mike Costache, went with him.

Then Sergei's buddy says something that doesn't have anything to do with women:

"Just so you know, Sergei works for the FBI."

Sergei is sitting right next to him. He doesn't say anything. He doesn't punch him on the shoulder and say, "Get the hell out of here!" or "That's B.S.!"

I've had my suspicions about Sergei, pretty much since we had drinks in the empty bar at the Andaz Hotel in New York. Those concerns increased when we met at Trump's Chicago hotel, and he offered to pay me thirty grand a month. Then there was his email about "men in black" in November. But this claim is bizarre. Sergei finally looked up at the ceiling—a classic, let's-change-the-subject-because-I-don't-want-to-deal-with-this-right-now look.

Is this a joke? A stupid prank floated by this weird guy who sounds like he's in the middle of a midlife crisis? I'm the odd man out here, and nobody is trying to help me get even by clarifying things. So I laugh it off.

We leave the Russia House, and the new guy leads us to a cafe to smoke hookah—Middle Eastern water pipes. He meets a young woman there, and she accompanies us back to their hotel. In the room, there are cameras and laptop computers lying around. When Sergei and his pal go get cigarettes, I close the laptops. When they return, I leave.

I don't think much about Sergei or his visit with McCain until three days later—when hell starts breaking loose.

THE MILLIAN QUESTION MAN

On January 24, 2017, as I'm thinking about my upcoming interview for a job with the Trump administration, I get one of the biggest shocks of my life.

The Wall Street Journal reports that Sergei Millian is the source behind the unverified allegations in the Steele Dossier linking Trump to Russia, including the document's most salacious claim of a compromising sex tape that could be used to blackmail Trump.

This guy, who wanted to be a big buddy of mine, who talked about setting up businesses with me, who told me he knew Michael Cohen, who was so eager to be a Trump insider, was talking trash about Russia and Trump?

The article reports that Millian, listed as both Source D and Source E in the dossier, made his shocking claims to an informant who relayed them to Steele.

In addition to the videotape charge, Millian also allegedly told the informant that there was a "conspiracy of cooperation" between the Trump camp and Russian leadership that involved hacking the computers of Mr. Trump's Democratic opponents.

I also learn that his real name is Siarhei Kukuts, that he had lived in Atlanta before moving to New York, and that his grandly named organization, the Russian-American Chamber of Commerce in the USA, averaged earnings and donations of less than $50,000 a year.

I'm in shock. I message him immediately. "Sergei I don't know what this is all about. I have nothing to do with Russia. I don't know what you're up to."

He messages me back: "I know."

That's the last I hear from him. Ever.

But I'm totally freaked out. Sergei's been blabbing to intelligence operatives. And not just any operative—to someone tied to a vast, frightening conspiracy theory that is right out of the movie *Manchurian Candidate*, where a foreign power gains control of an American president. If what he says is true, it's chilling on a national level. And if what he's quoted as saying in the Steele Dossier isn't true, the new administration will be crippled anyway by such horrifying allegations.

Meanwhile, on a personal level, it's pretty damning for me. I'm thinking, "Oh my God, I'm trying to get a job in the administration, and now this son of a bitch has been leaking and spinning to everyone.

If the administration learns I've been meeting this guy, I'm screwed—even though I've barely said a word to him about Russia, and I've turned down all of his overtures. The optics are deadly.

I recall that I did plan to try to introduce Millian to Trump senior advisor Boris Epshteyn, but I never pursued it. I hope that doesn't raise any flags.

In the meantime, I try to put on a brave face. I'm scheduled for a phone interview with someone handling administration jobs, who seems very intrigued about me joining the NSC or Department of Energy. I've been angling for a gig at the National Security Council or the Department of Energy. It's January in Chicago. I go to the gym. I meet friends for coffee.

I have two immediate concerns: not freezing my ass off and keeping my job hopes alive.

CHAPTER 10

MEN IN BLACK ATTACK

I'M AT MY mother's home in Chicago, shaving, on January 27, 2017, when my phone rings. It's from a number I don't recognize.

Probably a telemarketer and I'm going to wish I'd never picked up the damn phone, right?

It turns out to be worse.

A lot worse.

"This is the FBI. We are outside your house. We'd like to interview you."

My first thought is, "Really? Is this a joke?" Nobody but criminals should expect to get a phone call from the Feds, right? But the special agent on the end of the line sounds like the real thing, utterly deadpan. My experience with the FBI, at this point, is the same as 99% of all Americans: I only know what I've seen on TV and on the big screen.

The immediate thing that comes to mind, though, is that they probably want to talk to me about Sergei Millian.

"Sure, I can talk to you. Where are you?"

They answer by pounding on my front door. "FBI! Open up!"

I wipe the shaving cream off my face and answer the door, wrapped in a towel. In front of me are two special agents. Their names are Curtis Heide and Michael McSwain. They are from the Bureau's Chicago office.

"You know what we want to talk to you about," says Heide.

"I'm not sure exactly."

"Come on. You know we want to talk to you about your friend in New York."

"Yeah. I had an idea."

They tell me they want to ask me some questions and that I can be a great help to national security. Given all the crazy things that have happened to me over the last nine months, and the recent revelations about Millian, I am happy to help.

"We'd like you to come to our office."

"Why don't we talk here?"

"No. We can't talk here."

I don't feel like I have much of an option—I'm sure most people feel that way when the FBI comes calling. But the fact is, I have nothing to hide. They're just going to ask me about that idiot Millian. Plus, I want to get these guys out of my hair so I can gear up for talking to my White House contacts later that day. I go upstairs, put on a suit, and then get in their car.

Right away they began peppering me with questions about money:

"Why do you live in such an expensive area of Chicago, George?"

"It's my mother's house. She's in real estate. I'm getting ready to move, hopefully."

"Why do you dress so expensively?"

"I think I dress pretty normally. I like to wear jeans, too."

"You also travel a lot. Do you like living overseas?"

"Yes. I lived in London for a long time. I love it there."

"Yeah, London. We are definitely going to want to talk to you about that."

What the hell does that mean? I have no clue.

At one point, Curtis Heide turns around from the passenger seat to face me. His eyes narrow. "If you tell us the truth, you won't get in trouble."

Is that a warning? A threat? Cold-blooded advice? Maybe all three. It feels like a statement of fact with a definite undercurrent of hostility.

Now I wonder if I am some kind of target.

What the fuck have I done?

THE HEIDE CHRONICLES

I'm in a room inside the FBI's Chicago field office. I don't see any cameras or recording devices, but apparently, every word I say is taped. This is how I remember it:

The first thing they do is show me a black-and-white photo of Millian.

"Do you know this man?"

"Of course. That's Sergei Millian."

"How do you know him?"

I tell them Millian contacted me claiming he had done deals with Trump and that he thought he could help with the campaign. I say we met a number of times. And that he had some business proposals for me, but nothing had come of them.

"Was he trying to cultivate you?"

"Cultivate me?" I start to laugh. "I don't know what you mean."

The two agents look at each other.

"Well, George," Heide says, "that was just a ruse. We're not really that interested in talking to you about Sergei Millian. We have a lot more to talk about."

I don't say anything. I'm trying to weigh this information. Is that even true—that they don't care about Millian? And if it is true, does that mean Sergei's pal was telling the truth when he said to me that Sergei worked for the FBI? But why would Sergei talk about Russia with me if he was working for the United States? I have no clear read on what is going on.

Then Heide says: "We want to ask you about Russia."

"Look, guys, the reality is I have no serious contacts to Russia. All my contacts are in Israel."

I mention this to the agents because I wanted to show them just how off the mark they were. Did they really think I was working with Putin's people? I needed to convey to them that they were way off base.

"Well, let's talk about Israel."

"What do you want to know?"

"Did you meet with Aviv Ezra recently?"

Aviv Ezra is the Consul General of Israel to the Midwest, based in Chicago. He's like a surrogate ambassador for the middle of America. He has nothing to do with the campaign or anything that I can fathom.

"Yes. I've known Aviv for a while. We met when he was at the Ministry of Foreign Affairs. I went to his office to see him right after he got his appointment, just to catch up with him."

"What did you discuss?"

"General topics."

"Did they take your phone?"

"Yes. I left my phone with the security detail. You give them your phone before you walk in."

"Tell us more about the Israelis cultivating you."

"What do you mean cultivating? What's this word? 'Cultivating?' No one's cultivating me. I know many people in Israel. I know many people in various governments, but my relationships aren't 'cultivated.'"

"Your ties to that country bear scrutiny."

I don't say anything to that at first. I don't know what that means, but they seem to be implying something.

"It's interesting you think that, but I'm not a spy if that's what you're alleging." That gets no response. Instead, they keep things moving.

"Now let's talk about Russia and interference. Who in the campaign knew about interference?"

"I don't know what you're talking about."

"Who knew, George?"

"Come on, George!"

"I had nothing to do with Russian interference, and neither did anyone on the campaign as far as I'm aware."

"Will you answer questions about people in the campaign?"

"I don't think I have an issue with that. If someone was working with the Russians, I would love to help you guys figure it out."

This is true. I would be happy to help. I try to help. There are a few huge problems: The first is that I don't really know anything. The second is that most of my interactions regarding anything to do with Russia happened more than six months ago. So none of the precise details or timelines are fresh in my mind. And while I'm talking to them, I'm not consulting my email or calendar. I should point this out to Heide and McSwain—that I don't have total recall and they are asking me about timeline events as far back as the previous March—but I don't.

Big mistake.

"What did you know about Russian hacking or collusion?" says one G-man.

"Did you ever talk with a Russian government official?" says the other.

"I have never knowingly spoken with a Russian government official in my life," I say. All these Russia questions are making me a bit nervous. Russia, Russia, Russia. First Mifsud brought up Russia. Then Downer, Millian, Azra Turk, and Halper. I'm an expert on energy issues in the Mediterranean. But everyone wants me to be the go-to guy—or maybe the fall guy—when it comes to linking the Trump campaign to Putin.

I decide to tell them my one truly bizarre interaction of interest.

"You know what? There was this weird guy from Malta—Joseph Mifsud. He told me that the Russians have the goods on Hillary Clinton. He said they have dirt on her. They have thousands of emails from her."

This is my big reveal. I'm making eye contact with my inquisitors as I drop what should have been a bombshell revelation on them.

They don't blink. They don't budge. It was as if I'd told them two plus two equals four or that the sky is blue. So what else is new, George? I will never forget the lack of response or interest as long as I live. It's as if they already knew what Mifsud told me.

They ask no questions about how Mifsud knew anything about Russians and Clinton's emails. They never ask if I had pushed Mifsud for his sources or if he had shed any light on his sources. They also never ask about his failure to connect me to Russians. Or the logical extension of that unasked question: If he couldn't connect me to government officials, how was this clown in any position to know what the Russians did or didn't do?

But they do want to know when I met Mifsud and how often we talked. My memory is blurry. I tell them I met Mifsud before joining the campaign.

I was wrong. There's a difference between having a faulty memory and actively lying—or there should be. But there isn't when you are dealing with the FBI. I should have said: I don't remember.

They are even more interested in my motives for meeting Mifsud and whether he introduced me to any Russian people.

"He's a nobody." I definitely downplay Mifsud. Not because I feel implicated but because I feel embarrassed. My mindset is: he failed to introduce me to anyone of substance. He was a bullshitter. Why should I pretend he was a big shot or over-sell our interactions? He was a con artist.

"I didn't know if he was serious," I tell the investigators. "But he turned out to be a real nobody." Then I tell them about Mifsud introducing me to the young woman described to me as Putin's niece—and how that felt like a bizarre charade.

I also tell them it "isn't like Mifsud was messaging me in April while I'm with Trump." Again, I don't have my calendar open in front of me when I'm talking. I'm not scanning through my text messages either. I'm just trying to recall events as accurately as I can. I don't realize at this time that every statement I make to the FBI can, if I botch a single fact, be used as a lasso to snare me.

The interview ends. Neither agent seems very happy, as though I haven't been telling them what they want to hear. But there's nothing I can do about that. I can't deliver a smoking gun because, as far as I know, none exists.

They drive me back home and say they'll be in touch.

I don't even bother calling my contacts in Washington. My dream is over. I'm crushed. Nine months of work down the drain. So much time and energy—and yes, money—wasted. The FBI has made me a security risk. Nobody is going to hire me now. Instead, I'm going to be doing the hiring…I need a lawyer.

AN OFFER I REFUSE

A few days later, on January 31, I'm at the gym when I get a call from Curtis Heide. He peppers the conversation with lots of "bros."

"Hey, George, I'm not here to trip you up or anything, bro," he says in his best good cop act. "But can we meet and figure out what's going on?"

He wants to figure what's going on? That's a laugh. All of this is entirely new to me.

"Okay," I say. "Let's meet with my lawyer." I had just hired counsel the day before.

"No, no, no. Let's not get lawyers involved. This is just going to be a quick conversation between you and me, and then I'm not going to bother you again."

"I don't know."

"Come on, George."

"Okay," I say, acting like a total fool.

I realize now I should have told him to call my lawyer and hung up. But, as you've probably noticed, I often go with the flow—to my detriment.

We meet at George's Cafe in Andersonville, a vibrant neighborhood on Chicago's North Side, not far from my family home in Lincoln Square.

Heide sits down and looks out the window. His face is tight. I'm nervous, but he's agitated. Paranoid, even.

"Did you tell anyone that you were coming here?" he asks. "Did you tell anyone where you are? Are you being followed?"

He continues looking out the window.

"No," I say. "I just came from the gym."

Finally, he focuses on me. "George, I'm just letting you know that we want you to wear a wire."

"What?"

"A wire. We want you to work for us."

"A wire for what?"

"We want you to go to London and to get this guy Mifsud for us. We can pay you, and you can be a key part of an FBI operation. We will let you peek behind an FBI operation."

What the fuck am I supposed to say this? Am I supposed to be a hero now? Me? I'm a policy guy, a networker who wants to build alliances and energy deals. I admit, for a second, that part of me likes the idea of being a hero. But then I think, wait a minute! Two days ago these guys didn't seem to give a damn about Mifsud, really. They didn't ask anything specific about him. Instead of jumping on his revelation about Hillary's emails being hacked, it seemed pretty clear that they already knew all about him and what he had told me.

But what if Mifsud really was a Russian agent? Did I want to risk getting caught up with spies? Maybe I've seen too many movies but being a spy or wearing wires doesn't seem like a great way to achieve longevity.

"Look, I don't know what to tell you. This guy told me that they have Hillary's emails. I told you that. I don't know what more I can do. I haven't seen him or spoken to him in months. I wish you guys came to me sooner. Aren't you the professionals? What do you need me to wear a wire for?"

"To help us."

"I'll think about it. But I don't think my lawyers are going to want me to do this."

This proves to be a wrong answer. Suddenly, Heide turns from being my bro into my tormentor.

"I know everything about you," he says. It's meant as a threat, as if I've done something wrong and I'm going to pay for it. But I'm not sure what any of this means. I wrack my brain. Does he have an incriminating video of me jaywalking? Because, other than that, I can't think of any other legal transgressions I might have made.

"Look, Curtis, I'm trying to help you guys. But at this point, I don't even want to be involved in politics anymore. I just want to go to law school."

"I know."

"What do you know?"

"I know everything about you. I know you don't do drugs. I know you were dating Salma in London. I know your girlfriend was Naz. And I know you're at the center of this, and if you don't help us, we're going to bust your ass for what you're doing with Israel. You're lucky we're not doing it now because they're allies. But Washington wants answers, and Washington wants answers now."

I'm completely speechless as I try to process everything that's just happened. This frigging FBI agent is a yo-yo. He's playing good cop/bad cop by himself. One minute he's calling me "bro" and assuring me he's not here to trip me up. The next, he's asking me to wear wires. Then he's making these wild allusions to espionage charges. What the fuck?

I tell Heide I have to go. Outside, I start to panic. Israel? I have friends and associates who are Israeli, no question. But an Israeli also set me up with that jerk of an Australian High

Commissioner who was so hostile to me. So what the hell is going on? I call my lawyers. "There's something wrong here," I say. "Really wrong."

George Berbas, one of my three attorneys—the others are Robert Stanley and Tom Breen—tries to calm me down. He tells me the agency has been in contact with him. "They want you to come talk one more time," he says. "Let's get them out of our hair and just tell them what they want to know."

These guys are lawyers. I'm not. I've paid a $10,000 retainer for them to give me advice. I figure they know what they are doing. I agree.

ANOTHER SETUP

I meet with the FBI on February 16, 2017. This time it's not just Heide and McSwain. There's an entire armada of people—some of whom have flown in from Washington. One of the investigators is an FBI lawyer named Kevin Clinesmith. And he seems to be leading a lot of this inquisition.

Clinesmith is sitting across the table from me. And he asks the same question that Heide has already asked me a dozen times about Mifsud's Hillary Clinton email remark: "Who did you tell on the campaign?"

"I thought what Mifsud was telling me was bullshit, and I didn't share it with anyone on the campaign."

"Are you sure you didn't share it with anyone?"

"I didn't share with anyone on the campaign. No."

This is the only issue anybody seems to want to talk about. I keep waiting for someone to ask me about Mifsud himself. But nobody seems to care about him. I can't believe these people are not interested in the source of this information. Didn't they want to know how I met this guy, who introduced us, or what his background is?

I volunteer that Mifsud recently contacted me via Facebook and said he might be coming to America. They thank me for this information, and an agent asks me for Mifsud's and Olga's phone numbers and emails, which I provide.

Clinesmith says: "George, do you remember having drinks with a friendly Western diplomat at a bar in London?"

I burst out laughing. It's a ridiculous question. "I've had many drinks with many diplomats in many bars in London," I say. "I don't know who you're talking about."

He doesn't give any further information to help me narrow down the answer. Instead, he says, "Are you sure?"

It may seem obvious to the reader that Clinesmith was referring to Alexander Downer. But remember: this is more than nine months after I had my drink with Downer. And honestly, I don't recall blabbing about the emails to him—plus, as I already mentioned, Downer later confirms I never mentioned emails.

Under the onslaught of questions from these lawmen, I don't recall anything, and that's what I say: "I don't remember any specific meeting."

With that, Clinesmith and his team get up and storm out of the room. They don't even say thank you or goodbye. I give my lawyers a perplexed look, as if to say: That was strange. Who behaves like this?

They shrug.

Then, a couple of days later, my lawyer Tom calls.

"I have Kevin Clinesmith on the phone from Washington, one of the gentlemen that we met with a couple of days ago. He has a question to ask."

"Hello, Kevin," I say. "How's it going?"

"Do you remember meeting with Alexander Downer?"

"Yes. I met with him once."

Click. Clinesmith hangs up the phone.

Thinking back on this now, I imagine him slamming down the phone and dancing a jig in his office. In his aggressive, hostile, take-no-prisoners mind, he probably thought I had just substantiated Downer's claim and incriminated myself.

In a few months, it turns out, I'll be able to dance a jig about Clinesmith, too—when he is booted off the investigation for profoundly anti-Trump remarks. But I'm getting ahead of myself, again.

Right after the FBI meeting, I tell my lawyers I want to deactivate my Facebook account. I don't want Mifsud reaching out to me anymore. I don't want anyone reaching out to me at this point. I want to exist in a vacuum. I discuss it with them because I thought there might be problems with the perception that I was trying to destroy evidence. If I closed my account or deactivated it, for all I knew, some email or messages might get wiped out. My lawyers tell me to go ahead and do it. I shut my account.

Whew, I tell myself. I'm making it harder for Mifsud and others to get me.

But I've just made it easier for the FBI.

THE NET WIDENS

The next day I'm having brunch in Lincoln Square with one of my best friends, Omar Ahmed, when he answers a call on his phone. His eyes go wide, and he starts reciting what the person on the other end of the call is saying. "Yes, I know George Papadopoulos...Yes. He's a friend of mine...Sure. What's this about?...Okay, see you then."

"Holy shit," he says, ending the call. "That was the FBI. They want to come and meet me right now. And ask me some questions."

I don't know what to say.

I look at my phone. Another close friend, Jeffrey Wisemen, has been texting me frantically and leaves me a voicemail: "Bro. What the fuck is going on? The FBI was just at my house for two hours. They were questioning me about you and your life and your ties to Israel. They had surveillance photos of me and you at a casino together, and I don't know what's going on."

I call him back while Ahmed is still with me. "Guys," I say. "I don't know what's going on."

Jeff tells me that Curtis Heide asked him where I get my money. He says that Heide mentioned Jeff's half-Arab, half-Polish background and said, "Why do you stick up for George when he supports the Jews?"

"I don't know what's going on, man," Jeff says. "They were showing me articles about you and asking me everything about you."

My mind is racing, trying to process the best path forward. I'm also concerned now that anything I tell my friends could be considered meddling or obstruction. "Guys," I said, "I'm sorry. But I can't talk to you about this anymore."

The sad thing is, we haven't talked since that day. I hope we connect soon.

Later that day, my uncle calls me.

"The FBI was at my house and showed me surveillance photos of you walking on streets. They wanted to know where you get your money? I told them 'his father's a doctor and his mother's in real estate. He's not a poor person.'"

My friends start to disappear from my life. It's like I have social leprosy. I launch a new Facebook page and people decline my invitations.

I can't blame them. The FBI, as I've discovered the hard way, can turn your life into a living hell. And if they want, they can wreck your friends' lives, too. That's the power of federal investigators. The pursuit of justice gives lawmen a license to intimidate and destroy anyone in their path.

I realize I have no idea who the FBI has interviewed about me. Dozens of people may have been quizzed, but they haven't told me about it because they're probably scared to death.

On March 10, I receive an email notification from Gmail informing me that my email account has been hacked by a government entity.

I'm really in the crosshairs now. The FBI is after me. I wonder who else is spying on me. Then I realize I'm afraid to find out the answer.

CHAPTER 11

LOVE AMONG
THE RUINS

A S SUDDENLY AS they appear, the FBI agents vanish from my life.

That's both good and bad. I don't know if I'm still in their sights or what they are digging up on me. That's another thing about having the Bureau zero in on you. You are expected to answer their questions, but they don't answer yours.

So I'm nervous. I'm jittery. I have no clue what the future holds for me. Career-wise, I'm rudderless. The idea of working for the administration is, I now believe, completely shut to me. I have one distraction: A crush.

Months earlier, while I was networking on LinkedIn, I noticed the London Centre of International Law Practice had added a new member to the staff. Actually, to be entirely accurate, I noticed the LCILP had added a really pretty young woman. In fact, I thought she was stunning. I clicked on her profile and scoured it for more information. She had started working there in September. We had missed each other by about five months! I couldn't believe it. More bad timing.

Her résumé was as intriguing as her picture. She was from Italy. She had studied law. She had worked for Versace! And she had spent the last seven years working for the president's office of the European Parliament—a place that had interested me for years.

I reached out to her.

"I see you work at the Centre. I recently left there. Judging by your picture, which is great, I obviously left too early."

Simona says she initially thought I was hitting on her, and of course, I was. But she also says she looked at my profile and thought I was cute. And make no mistake, I was flirting, but I wasn't sending her some crass, Tinder-style come-on.

She wrote back.

I was instantly intrigued by this gorgeous, politically aware, globally conscious international lawyer who spoke Italian, French, German, English, and Spanish, and had a great sense of humor. To me, she was something out of a movie, or a dream. Then I found out that she actually acted in movies— and was even going to the Cannes Film Festival.

There was no end to the surprises with this dazzling blonde from Caserta, near Naples, raised by a university professor and an ESL teacher.

She even knew Joseph Mifsud.

Yeah. I know. You can't make this stuff up.

She met Mifsud in about 2012. At the time, she was working as an attorney on child abduction cases in Brussels for the European Parliament. Italian politician Gianni Pittella, a member of the parliament, introduced Mifsud to her. She said the two men were frequently together. And that while she understood Pittella's position—he became president of the Socialists and Progressive Democrats and served as one of fourteen vice presidents of the European Parliament—she didn't know that much about Mifsud. Sometimes Mifsud—acting in his professorial mode—would bring students to Brussels. As she understood it, he was well connected to Italy's politicians, taught at Link Campus Rome, and also worked in London.

In 2016, she was looking for new opportunities when Pittella suggested that she work with Mifsud who, he said, was a senior member of the London Centre of International Law Practice.

Like me, Simona loves London. So she moved there to start work at the Centre. She was quickly disenchanted. There was no law to practice. She didn't understand why Mifsud had hired her, although she began to think it was because he wanted to access her extensive European contacts.

Simona and I progressed from LinkedIn to email to texting. And we tried to find a common time and place to meet. But every time, something would come up. I had the inauguration. She had conferences. It was always something. Finally, she told me she was coming to New York in April to visit with an aunt. "Great," I said, "what flight are you taking?"

I go to New York and pick her up at JFK Airport. What can I say? I am already crazy about her. She says she has mixed feelings about me being there to greet her. Why? Because no woman wants to meet a potential suitor for the first time after an eight-hour transatlantic flight. You don't exactly look your best, she says.

Well, she looks fantastic to me. We go straight to dinner. Our connection is absolutely electric. I can't take my eyes off this vibrant, brilliant beauty. She is outspoken, opinionated, passionate about the world. And gorgeous. I am completely smitten.

She's only in town a few days—and she has to see her aunt—but I spend every hour I can with her. I tell Simona a bit about the FBI. I'm a little embarrassed about it and about the sudden turns my life has taken. She's a sympathetic listener. She is also, I think, happy that I am not working for Trump. Her politics are to the left of mine.

I learn from her that Nagi and Mifsud had mentioned me when they were wooing her to join the LCILP. They told her she needed to meet this guy who was Trump's advisor. He just quit the Centre to work with the campaign. Stuff like that. She also tells me how, her first day there, they slapped her picture at the top of the website—so she was sandwiched in between Nagi and Mifsud, like some senior bigwig with an important title.

"They didn't even ask me. I don't understand what this organization does. I was worried about my reputation."

"Join the club," I say. "That place is crazy."

"I know. I'm a lawyer. I never once discussed a case with anyone there! There was something so wrong with that place."

She even fired off an email in October 2016, after two months on the job, saying she felt Mifsud had tricked her into working for free.

He gave a typical shadowy, ignore-the-facts response, writing in Italian:

> Dear Simona,
> I hope you are fine...I was in Moscow...Now I'm in London. Can we meet in person? I'm here until Tuesday night.
> A hug.
> J

A hug? Really?
She says that was the last time they communicated.

It is therapeutic for both of us to share our confusion and frustration with the LCILP. Is it a spy recruitment center? A think tank? A tax shelter? We have no idea.

But we don't spend too much time dwelling on it. I guess you could say we dwelled on each other.

ANOTHER INTRODUCTION

During my days with the Trump campaign, I was contacted by an Israeli named David Ha'ivri, a conservative strategist who works for West Bank settlers.

During the March 2017 AIPAC conference in D.C., Ha'ivri contacts me and says there's an American-Israeli businessman who wants to meet me. His name is Charles Tawil.

"I'm happy to meet with you," I say.

They fly out to Chicago, and I arrange a lunch at Shallots, a popular kosher steakhouse in Skokie, a Chicago suburb with a large Jewish population. It sounds like Tawil might lead to work. I'm broke. I've got legal bills. I'll take any consulting gig I can get. But I'm also suspicious. These guys just flew out to meet me without any specific agenda. That seems slightly strange.

Ha'ivri is tall, bearded, and wears a skullcap. He's in his late forties, maybe. Tawil is bald, wears glasses and looks about sixty, I guess. He's wearing a suit and a bold red tie. Should these looks tell me anything? No. But after my FBI grilling, I'm much more guarded. Tawil isn't.

"It's so good to finally meet you!" he says. "I'm so glad David could put this together because I've been trying to get ahold of you since you spoke at the Hadera Energy Conference"—which I attended in April 2016—"but Israeli intelligence wouldn't let me get near you."

Israeli intelligence? Is he telling me he's tight with Mossad or Shin Bet? I have never had anything to do with Israeli intelligence. My guard goes up further.

Then he shifts the subject. "Obviously a Greek Orthodox guy like you has close ties to Russia. You were probably viewed as a middleman with Trump and Russia just simply based on those characteristics."

Ten minutes into our meeting and he's swung things to Russia. What the hell? I don't say anything. And his geopolitical survey of the State of Things moves on: "What NATO did to Serbia was a horrible thing," he says, before checking off other known Trumpian talking points—some of which Corey Lewandowski and I put forth in Trump's first foreign policy speech: the Islamist containment problem, China's multiple threats, the wisdom of working with Russia. I wonder if he's regurgitating this stuff because he has read a profile on me or if he is trying to profile me himself and see how I will respond.

Then Tawil starts sharing a bit about his work and connections in Africa and how he uses David to bring evangelical congressmen to certain African countries to meet with their leaders. But he's noticeably short on specifics other than dropping the name of former South African president Jacob Zuma. By the time we've finished eating, I feel like I've learned nothing and achieved nothing. As far as I can tell, Charles Tawil has just spent at least $2000 flying to Chicago and taking me to lunch and flying back to D.C. or Israel. Actually, if he is paying Ha'ivri for his time as a consultant, the whole thing must have cost a lot more. Why? Because he liked a speech I gave at a conference? It doesn't make a lot of sense to me.

We go outside. Charles suggests I stand by David so he can take a picture. Great. Another picture. Am I that interesting looking? Or does a dossier somewhere need a new photograph?

CONGRATULATIONS: YOU ARE UNDER SURVEILLANCE

On April 12, 2017 I get an email out of the blue from a reporter at a national press outlet: "Mr. Papadopoulos I've been meaning to reach out to you for a long time. It's very important for us to meet."

I respond that I'm happy to talk and suggest we arrange a time.

The very next day I get a message from Rhonda Schwartz, the head of investigations at ABC News in New York. She tells me it's very important that we meet because she has something to discuss. She urges me to contact her immediately.

I try to stay calm. Two investigative reporters have just reached out to me. What do they want to talk about? What stories are they working on? Have they been talking to the FBI? Has someone been talking trash about me? These moments are so conflicted—I know I've done absolutely nothing wrong, and yet I can't help feeling that I'm a magnet for trouble—as if scumbags and spies are drawn to me. It is hard not to feel paranoid. I try to remember what a friend of mine calls the informed neurotic's anthem: "If you're not worried, you're not thinking."

I meet the reporter who called first at a cafe near Dupont Circle and he's brought a colleague with him. They tell me they've learned that I've been targeted by a FISA warrant as part of Robert Mueller's investigation into allegations of Trump-Russia collusion.

"I don't know why on earth I would have a FISA warrant on me," I say, before launching into my broken-record sound bite. "I don't have any contacts with Russia. I mean, I was just in the energy business and worked with Israelis."

As soon as the word "Israel" is out of my mouth, I see the reporters exchange a look. We talk for a while, but when they start pressing me on my relationship with Sergei Millian, I really don't feel comfortable talking anymore. I leave. I feel pretty shaken.

FISA warrants are issued by the Foreign Intelligence Surveillance Court, an eleven-man tribunal that works in secret. Each judge is able to approve requests to wiretap subjects suspected of spying with or for a foreign government. An approved warrant—which is essentially a rubber stamp, as the court denies only a tiny fraction of requests—gives a government agency the ability to wiretap a "foreign power or an agent of a foreign power" (which can include American citizens) suspected to be engaged in espionage or terrorism. It also allows for "bulk collection," meaning agents can collect the communications of other Americans who come in contact with a target.

I read more about FISA warrants. They are spy-all-you-want cards for investigators involved in foreign intelligence security. They allow the FBI, the CIA, and the DOJ to track a suspect's activities anywhere and any way. That means all my email, all my texts, all my phone calls are probably under surveillance. I think about my hacked Gmail account. It was probably the FBI exercising its FISA. I had called Curtis Heide to let him know about the hack—but he was probably the guy who initiated it. If it wasn't completely frightening, it would have been funny.

I call my lawyers and tell them what the two reporters told me. They say they will try to look into it. But there's not a lot they can do. FISA targets are secret for a reason: authorities are trying to dig up dirt on you.

I head to New York to meet Rhonda Schwartz in her ABC News office. She's very personable. After our friendly chit-chat, she says, "You seem like a very nice guy. I can't believe what I've heard about you. I hope it's not true."

"What are you talking about?"

"There's a FISA warrant on you?"

I can't believe I'm hearing this again. I tell her that I have no serious connections to Russia. Then Brian Ross, ABC's chief investigative reporter, comes in.

"Do you know if your bank or phone records have been subpoenaed?"

"I have no idea."

"You should look into it."

At the beginning of May 2017, Jim Wolfe, director of security of the Senate Select Committee on Intelligence (SSCI), calls me. The committee wants documents from me. If I don't provide them, I will get subpoenaed. I have no objection—other than that this feels like harassment. But I have nothing to hide, and I tell him that. A few days later, the subpoena arrives. It's unnecessary. They can have my so-called campaign-related communications regarding Russia, or anything else. I'm clean. All I want to do is spend time with Simona, who is back in London, and put this Russia nonsense behind me. So I ask my lawyers to get my travel documents back and make sure I'm not breaking any restrictions by going to Europe to live my life.

I'm at the airport, about to fly to Greece, when a group of armed guards stop me. I'm already through immigration and the security check, ready to board the plane. Four guys in military fatigues, black Kevlar, gripping assault rifles, pull me aside.

"Are you planning on returning to the United States?"

"Of course. This is my home."

"Are you planning on traveling anywhere else besides Greece?"

"Not at the moment. Why are you stopping me? Is this about Trump?"

"You're very young to have been working for Trump."

They ask to look through my bags. They take my phone. They ask for contact information for my family in Greece. I'm there for half-an-hour answering questions. At no time do they identify themselves to me. Finally, someone who looks like a representative from the airline comes over and tells them I need to get on the plane. They give me back my phone, my bags, and I'm on my way. I am completely relieved, and at the same time, I'm enraged. Now mysterious military guys are shaking me down?

FANTASY ISLAND

"Andreas, my life has been turned upside down."

I'm talking to my pal Andreas Papakyriakopoulos, the communications chief of the Greek government. It's the middle of May, and we are in a popular tavern in central Athens. I launch into everything that's happened in the last few months, and then I look over at the next table. A guy is eating alone. He has a beard. He's middle-aged. Is he a cop? A spy. I've just been told by two separate reporters that there's a warrant allowing the government to spy on my every action. I can't tell if I'm paranoid or just engaged in a completely rational self-defense strategy.

Who am I going to trust now? I don't even know if I can trust my good friend Andreas. He's connected to the government. Maybe they were tipped off, and they're actually surveilling me. It's an awful moment when you descend into this mindset. It's like a form of madness. Andreas pulls out his phone. Right away, I clam up for a moment. Is he taping me? Should I ask him? Instead of having a moment of clarity, where I unburden myself and share my nightmare, I'm adding to it. I leave dinner feeling everything in my life is falling apart.

I need to go on some R&R to the beach.

Super Paradise Beach in Mykonos.

With Simona.

Mykonos is a beautiful island. According to Greek mythology, it was formed out of the petrified bodies of giants killed by Hercules. Now it is a cosmopolitan giant of the European party scene, rivaling Ibiza and Majorca as a premier beach-bacchanalia destination. The world's top DJs fly in for thumping dance parties throughout the summer. The island's coastal coves create ideal private party spaces, so the dance-till-dawn revelries are sort of contained.

I have good friends who work at the bar on Super Paradise Beach. When I show up at the end of May, it's still the low season. So it's actually quite a chilled-out scene, which is what I want. My room is right above the beach. After a winter in Chicago, this is blissful. But the second day I'm there, I go downstairs to enjoy some surf and suds, and a friend at the bar says, "You know, you are being watched."

Eventually, I turn around to survey my surroundings. There are four American-looking guys dressed in black and wearing sunglasses, staring at the empty beach. We are the only people there. Again, I might be paranoid. But hey, these guys don't even have bathing suits on.

I thank my friend for pointing this out. Maybe I'm not entirely paranoid if other people notice that I have people following me. Still, I decide I'm not going to do anything differently. I'm here to get away from all the pressure.

While I'm waiting for Simona to arrive, I meet Kostas Skagias, who is the PR giant of Mykonos, the guy who handles most of the VIPs who come to party or lead the party on the island. It turns out I now qualify as a mini-celebrity. When I meet the minister of tourism, he pours on praise. "You're Papadopoulos! We love you! We are crazy about you. It's so great that you're working for Trump."

It's funny to me that, at least to some people, I still shine in the reflective glow of working on the Trump campaign. Meanwhile, in real life, that glow sometimes morphs into a dark shadow for me. I explain that I no longer work for Trump, but that it was a hell of an experience—an experience that, at the moment, I'm trying to forget by focusing on the dazzling parties of the island.

Kostas and I zip around the island, going from fashion shows to discos. It's a moveable feast filled with eccentric people, from models to millionaires to the flamboyant mayor of Mykonos. I have a great time. It's party therapy. If anyone is still monitoring me, I hope they are having a miserable time watching me have a great one.

While I'm in Mykonos, Simona is in another fabulous coastal playland—the Cannes Film Festival. She's been cast in *Affairs on Capri,* a film about English writer and ladies' man Graham Greene (who worked and wrote about British intelligence). Simona plays French sex symbol Brigitte Bardot, one of Greene's many love interests, in the film. The producer/director brings her to the festival to announce the film as he arranges for financing. She finally flies in to Mykonos. Once again, I pick her up at the airport. And things are great. The party continues as Kostas shepherds us to his favorite nightspot, Bao's, a waterfront cocktail bar in the beautiful Little Venice section of the island. We hang out on the yacht of Paris Latsis, the zillionaire shipping heir who was once engaged to Paris Hilton.

When we're not sipping champagne and sampling caviar, we're on the beach. There's a lot to talk about. I tell her about the FBI and all my nightmares—so much of which started with the London Centre of International Law Practice and our mutual acquaintance Professor Mifsud. We spend time discussing the Maltese man of mystery.

Fortunately, Simona finds the whole FBI investigation intriguing. I'm a pretty earnest guy. So being in the crosshairs of an international scandal adds a level of excitement and craziness that she finds attractive on some level.

She also tells me about her family history. Since I've known her, people invariably assume Simona is Russian. This false assumption arises, in part, from so many media reports tying her to Mifsud and the whole Russia-collusion story. She's also very blonde—which I guess is more common for Russians than Italians. Finally, she speaks five languages, so her accent is inevitably shaped by so many different tongues and may seem Slavic to some listeners. At any rate, it is stunning how many people think she's a Muscovite. The truth is, her mother Carolina is from a little village near Salerno on the Amalfi Coast, where she grew up among vast olive groves. The family was prosperous enough to send Simona's blue-eyed and blonde grandmother, Concetta Barba, to college in Genoa. Carolina, Concetta's daughter, studied languages. Simona, the youngest of three children, adores her mother and credits her for helping shape her open, adventurous, caring worldview. Her father, Giovanni Mangiante, spent part of his childhood in Lucerne, Switzerland, as his mother is Swiss. He is a classics professor and college administrator who has also worked in tourism development. Simona's parents believed in focusing their children on academics. Although Simona was always, as she says, very girlie, she was not allowed to have a boyfriend until she was eighteen.

Our moment of bliss is interrupted by a message from Charles Tawil. He wants to know where I am and then says he wants to see me in Mykonos to discuss working together. I don't get the urgency. I tell him I'm on vacation with my girlfriend and ask if this can wait.

He provides the answer by flying in.

Charles has subsequently given interviews saying I wanted to see him and that we had a warm relationship. But think about this: his trip to Mykonos marked the second time he had flown a considerable distance at his own expense to see me. Why? The other thing to remember—which I did not know at the time—was that documents published on WikiLeaks revealed Tawil was a secret American intelligence asset who provided information in South Africa. Here's an excerpt from the cable the US ambassador sent to the Central Intelligence Agency, Defense Intelligence Agency, National Security Council, and secretary of state:

> This in part, coincides with another Embassy contact, Charles Tawil (protect), who told our Economic Counselor on November 29 that Zuma had received information from the mother of the King of Swaziland about CIA attempts to kill Zuma using poisoned clothes from the FBI.

Despite this and all his many other allusions to spying—not to mention the fact that he made his approach to someone facing financial duress, a classic spycraft move—he denies working in intelligence. It goes without saying, however, that intel operatives generally don't raise their hands and admit to spying. Add those things up, and his sudden intense interest in me seems more than a little strange.

When Tawil shows up, I think this is pretty weird. But I message him to come out with me, Simona, and Kostas. He seems uncomfortable talking around them. On the occasions we do talk, he's just not making sense to me—I don't really understand his business proposal, although he seems to want me to go on a business trip with him.

I keep asking him: "What is it you want me to do?"

"Sometimes you get money just to stand next to certain people," he tells me. I think this is a very bizarre job requirement. But Charles seems unperturbed. "I have faith in you, George. I'm going to be paying you, and we're going to figure something out. I know that you're going to be a great asset."

"An asset to what?" I say. Does he mean intelligence "contact"—like he was described in that leaked cable? That spooks me.

He starts selling himself to me, talking about how he's lived in South Africa. How he's friends with the president of Uganda, Yoweri Museveni, a guy who has ruled with an iron fist for thirty years. He also starts talking to me about Jonathan Pollard, the convicted American intelligence analyst who provided suitcases filled with classified documents to Israeli operatives in return for tens of thousands of dollars, jewelry, and paid vacations. Pollard served thirty years in prison before being released. Tawil says he knew Pollard's handler and that "it wasn't our fault he got caught." This creeps me out even more. I'm not here to discuss spies or spycraft or intelligence operations.

Finally, he invites me to come to Israel to meet some people and continue discussions. I still don't get it. But Tawil clearly has money to fly all over the place, and he professes to want my help. It may sound stupid of me to agree to go. I'm growing suspicious of the guy, especially with his stories about Pollard and "advising" African presidents. The word Simona uses to describe him is "shady." Despite those misgivings, I need work, and I know nothing about his intelligence background.

Tawil says, I need you guys to come to Tel Aviv.

When I ask Simona if she wants to go, she says, "That doesn't make any sense. Why do you have to go there when he's already here?"

It's an excellent question. But Tawil insists. He keeps talking about me working with him in "government consulting," and that he has people he wants me to meet.

He flies back to Israel. I agree to join him there, and I tell him I'll need a contract and a retainer. Simona and I have a few more days to enjoy each other's company. She is extremely positive about our future and invites me to Italy. When we say goodbye, my plan is to join her there—and maybe even meet her family. I'm over the moon.

MONEY MATTRESS

I fly to Israel a few days later, and Tawil takes me to a meeting with Shai Arbel, an ex-Israeli intelligence officer, who talks about a program his company Terrogence runs that the CIA and the FBI use to monitor social media manipulation. Stuck in the room with Tawil and these cyber warriors, I wonder if I'm being framed. I remember Curtis Heide telling me he "knew all about Israel." Am I being recorded and entrapped?

The meeting ends and Tawil and I go out to eat. He tells me that he was one of seven agents who worked on an operation to tap the phones of Syrian president Hafez al-Assad, the father of current Syrian strongman Bashar al-Assad. "We could have killed him at any time." He also tells me again about his great friendship with former South African president Jacob Zuma—and he doesn't seem bothered in the least that the man is regarded as a completely corrupt profiteer (as of this writing, he's currently facing multiple counts of corruption, money laundering, and racketeering).

None of this impresses me. In fact, it irritates me. Why is he telling me this? I remember an expression I once heard describing a guy who couldn't stop bragging about his achievements: He can't keep it in his pants. That sort of fits Tawil. But there's something else that bothers me about his stories. It's like he's telling me he has special connections everywhere. If that is the case, what does he need me for?

We go to a hotel near Tel Aviv. For some reason, he books a room in that very same hotel, even though I'm pretty sure he lives in Tel Aviv. Why does he need a room? I don't ask, but I have a creepy feeling. In fact, I text Simona, who had a worse response to meeting Tawil than I had.

"How do I get out of here? This guy is so weird. I think I might be in danger."

Then he calls and says I should drop by his room. I'm completely nervous. Why his room? Why not the lobby? It seems like some kind of setup. Am I going to get whacked? I take a deep breath and tell myself that at least Simona knows where I am. That's good. She's my backup if, for whatever reason, something goes wrong.

Tawil opens the door to his room, and I step in. There's a pile of cash on the bed—a stack of what look like $100 bills.

"Ten thousand dollars," Tawil tells me.

"What's this for?"

"It's for you."

"Why? What am I doing for this money? I still don't understand our project."

"It's a retainer. You're working as my consultant."

"Why cash?"

"Why not?"

"We need an agreement."

"No, I trust you."

But I don't trust him. What kind of businessman gives someone $10,000—in cash—without a receipt or a contract? A terrible one, someone used to paying bribes, or a businessman who is not really a businessman.

Later, Tawil told reporters I asked for cash because I didn't have a bank account, which is just a lie. He also explained the cash by saying, "I have cash. I work in Africa, you know. I need cash." So which is it? Did I ask for cash? Or did he just have cash lying around that he wanted to use? Nice cover story.

In the end, I take the money. But I am scared. I've never seen $10,000 in cash before. And seeing it in Israel, on a bed in a hotel room in Israel is even stranger. Am I being taped? Is that Tawil's receipt—something he can use as blackmail that might lead to my undoing? Or is he going to finally give me what I've repeatedly asked for: an agreement, a contract, a statement of work. That's what I'm hoping for, something that explains where this money comes from, why I have it, and what is expected of me.

I make it through a night of restless sleep, wondering if I'm going to be the subject of a police raid. The next day, on June 9, we fly to Cyprus and drive to an out-of-the-way, remote town. I'm surprised. Every time I've been to Cyprus, I've stayed at the Hilton in Nicosia, where the business community congregates. Instead, we drive to a small village and Tawil pays a Vietnamese woman in cash for our rooms. This makes zero sense to me. The only thing I can think of is that we're here because it's near a meeting place. But that's not the case. Maybe it's easier to plant bugs in some out-of-the-way apartment than in a hotel room.

We continue having strange conversations. Driving to a meeting, Tawil tells me the money he gave me is made up of marked bills. He says I should get used to the cash, and I can make lots more of it by introducing people to Jared Kushner and others. Again, he's spewing complete fantasyland B.S. since he knows I'm not working for the Trump administration. He must be trying to entrap me. I say less and less.

I fly to Thessaloniki in the middle of June to attend a trilateral energy summit with Benjamin Netanyahu and the Greek and Cypriot presidents. I've still got the suitcase with $10,000 in it, and I still don't know why I have it. Given the amorphous discussion in Cyprus with Tawil's associate; the fact that Tawil's bizarre solicitations started immediately after the FBI put me in their sights; and the inexplicable mountain of cash given to me when a simple certified check would have sufficed, I smell a rat.

Or maybe a couple of rats. I do not trust Tawil.

So I drop the money off with a lawyer I know in Thessaloniki and get a receipt for it. To me, this is like putting the money in escrow until I figure out whether Tawil is a legitimate businessman or some kind of operative trying to set me up. Since I just spent a few days attending his bizarre meetings in Israel and Cyprus, I feel like I'm owed some money, but I'm not sure how much nor if the money is marked and will get me in trouble. So leaving it with a lawyer seems like the smartest thing to do.

My vacation is winding down, but first I spend more time with Simona. In Naples I meet her family. We visit the isle of Capri, where she is set to film her role in the movie. Then we jet back to Greece. I introduce her to some of my relatives. Eventually, it is time for me to go back to the States. I have an interview scheduled with John Moody, the executive vice president of Fox News, to discuss joining the network. After so many ups and down with the campaign, my summer in Europe has been exhilarating. I am head over heels in love with Simona. That was the R&R I wanted the most, and it happened. Even though long-distance relationships are tough, I'm determined to make this work. I get on a plane to Munich. Then I hop a connection to D.C. where I plan to make a connection to Chicago. I'm ready to move ahead and take a big leap with Simona. Where and when we will land, I'm not sure yet—Chicago? L.A.? D.C.? Brussels? I have no idea. But it's on.

Until it isn't.

CHAPTER 12

THE ARREST

I GET OFF my Lufthansa flight at Washington Dulles International Airport on July 27 and head toward immigration and customs so I can get my bags and then check in to my connection to Chicago.

But there's a slight hitch.

I'm texting with Simona to let her know I've landed when I spot a guy in a dark suit with a familiar look. The dark suit of a G-man. He's scanning the parade of departing passengers and locks his eyes on me. Am I surprised? Not really. I had told Simona about the military guys who shook me down on my way to Mykonos, and I feel like there's a possibility I'll get the third-degree from someone when I arrive. After all, I seem to be a person of interest.

"There's someone looking at me," I start texting Simona. "I think I'm going to be questioned."

"George Papadopoulos."

"Yes."

"FBI." He flashes a badge. Other agents fall in behind him.

"Follow me, George."

I send my text to Simona.

They lead me to a private area with at least a half-dozen FBI agents there, including Curtis Heide and Michael McSwain, who interviewed me in Chicago. I guess they are finishing what they started.

My briefcase is taken from me. So is my phone. My thoughts are fragmented. They come fast and furious. Oh my God, Simona has got to be wondering what happened to me. What do these guys want? Should I call my lawyers? Why is my backpack here? And how did it appear just five minutes after we landed? That's the FBI's new motto: We always get your bags! I need my phone; I should call Simona. Why are they looking through my bags? This is harassment! I haven't done a fucking thing! They just want to bring down Trump, right? That's all this is... They want me to say things that aren't true...I'm going to miss my connecting flight...What the hell are they looking for?

And then, finally, it dawns on me as they are going through my bags: Charles Tawil and the money.

They are looking for $10,000 in undeclared cash! That fucking guy was setting me up.

And quite probably, these guys are setting me up. Otherwise, what are they looking for? My vacation wardrobe? Are they interested in the SPF of my sunscreen? A bottle of ouzo? I have nothing of interest to anyone. Even to me!

So they must be looking for the money. But how do they know about the money? They must have read my texts to Simona and Tawil. Or they are working with Tawil.

Either that, or they are just trying to scare the hell out of me.

They put me in handcuffs and leg shackles and tell me I am under arrest.

They don't tell me why.

If the point is to scare the hell out of me, it works.

DEPARTURE DELAY

I'm at the airport for hours. The agents are texting and talking on the phone. I get the sense something didn't go as planned—like finding me with $10,000. I mean, really, if I'm under arrest, then take and book me. But that doesn't happen.

I'm shuffled into a black SUV with tinted windows. We go to a nearby detention center. I'm handcuffed to a wall. They get me some food.

Heide and McSwain come to talk to me.

"George, let's get this going," Heide says. "Let's get this show on the road right now. We don't need lawyers. We have two backpacks full of information about you."

They want me to talk right now. But it's an empty threat. I know there is nothing of relevance in my backpack or anywhere—unless they've planted something on me.

"Screw that. Get me my lawyers," I say.

Now it's nearly midnight. They take my phone. They ask me for the passcode to access it. I tell them to ask my lawyers for it. I sure as hell am not giving it to them.

I'm taken back to the SUV with tinted windows. I guess they've figured out a charge to process me on.

ROUGH JUSTICE

The FBI motto isn't actually "We always get your bags." It's Fidelity, Bravery, Integrity. Integrity, however, is not a word I would use in relation to my dealings with the Bureau's investigators. Under the direction of Special Counsel Robert Mueller, the former FBI head who is leading the probe into Russian interference in the 2016 presidential election, they are, in my experience, mean, nasty, and underhanded.

I have no memory of anyone reading me my Miranda rights at the airport. Agents asked me questions without the presence of my lawyer, who I said I wanted to speak to. When I said I wanted to let my girlfriend and family know what was happening, I was taunted and presumed guilty: "This is what happens when you work for Trump," one of the agents snarled at me. Nobody made an effort to get me to a phone—although I was eventually put in touch with my lawyers, who seemed to know more than I did.

Mueller's team makes a number of other high-profile arrests in its investigation into Russian influence after I was taken in: Paul Manafort, Manafort associate Rick Gates, Manafort lawyer Alexander van der Zwaan, Michael Flynn, Trump lawyer Michael Cohen, and Richard Pinedo. But none of them were pulled off a plane and hustled to prison after midnight for the charge of lying to the FBI. Manafort, Flynn, and Cohen all faced far more devastating charges than what I was hit with—and yet, they were all treated with relative decorum when it came time to get booked. They weren't threatened and taunted. And as far as I know, the FBI didn't use informants like Stefan Halper or Charles Tawil to entrap them. They were able to find paper trails and corroborating witnesses to put pressure on these profiteering Trump associates.

But when it came to Papadopoulos who cooperated fully with investigators? Let's arrest him in some kind of dramatic fashion.

A number of people have commented about the excessive behavior of the FBI in my case. Investigators knew who my lawyers were. They could have easily contacted them and asked me to come in. Or served me an indictment in the middle of the day when I arrived in Chicago. I wasn't a top-level player in the Trump campaign. And I wasn't a player in any kind of conspiracy, so I wasn't actually a flight risk. But none of this mattered to the prosecution team. I found out later that agents called my lawyers as my plane was landing and informed them of my arrest.

So much for courtesy calls.

It's also worth noting that I'm not the first to accuse Agent Michael McSwain of being overly aggressive. McSwain has been the object of a civil suit—*Aleynikov v. McSwain et al*, US District Court, District of New Jersey, No. 15-01170—that has been winding its way through court for years. Aleynikov alleges McSwain confiscated his passports and property illegally.

The rough behavior continues that evening. I'm driven to the city detention center in Alexandria, Virginia. My mug shot is taken well after midnight. I'm tossed in prison cell #113, which has a mattress on the floor and a huge guy as my cellmate and lights that never dim. I spend the night trying to sleep with one eye open, my mind spinning out of control.

Here's the thing: If I had been caught smoking pot or robbing a bank, then I'd know why I was in jail. It's simple logic: commit a crime, get caught, go to jail. But at this point, I still don't understand what I've done. I think it involves Trump and Russia. And that could mean anything. It could even, somehow, mean treason. And that is terrifying to think about—facing the unknown and all the worst-case scenarios is a form of torture. What do they have? Who did I meet? What bullshit witnesses have they found?

While I'm trying to process this, the cops toss a drunk into the cell. I'm treated to the sickening sights and sounds of him puking his guts out. I don't think I get more than an hour of sleep.

The next morning around 8:30, I'm dragged to my arraignment. My lawyers are in Chicago. I have no legal representation.

I'm told we are scheduled for a 9:30 a.m. hearing where I'm finally going to learn the charges against me. But Mueller's dream-team lawyers are delayed. These prosecutors are supposedly the cream of the crop when it comes to fighting crime and using the courts. How is it that they are holding up the show? What's the delay?

I wonder if they had been planning to use the $10,000 from Tawil to hit me with finance or smuggling charges or even spying charges or whatever entrapment plan they were hatching. If that is the case, now they have to scramble and find other charges.

When they get to court, they tell the magistrate I'm accused of two crimes: Lying to an FBI agent and obstructing justice. The prosecutors—one of them is Jeannie Rhee, a former deputy assistant attorney general for the Barack Obama administration from 2009 to 2011—say I'm looking at twenty-five years in prison.

This is not happening. This can't be happening. Lying? What did I say? Obstruction? What did I do?

Prosecutors tell the court I lied to Special Agent Curtis Heide. Apparently, I told him that I wasn't in contact with Mifsud in April of 2016—something to the effect of, "It's not like I'm messaging him when I'm with Trump in April." It turns out I emailed Mifsud once in that time span. No doubt as I was trying to arrange a meeting that never happened.

What a devastating lie! The entire future of democracy was jeopardized by my failure to recall a single, meaningless email!

For God's sake.

As for the obstruction charge, which is the one that carries serious jail time, it has to do with the fact that I deleted my Facebook account—which my lawyers told me I could do!

I'm trying to keep it together. I've barely slept in two days. I'm wearing the same shirt that I left Athens in. I smell like garbage. I look like garbage. I'm disoriented—because while I've just finally heard the charges, I still don't really understand any of it.

What is truly hard to understand is a prison sentence of twenty-five years. Is that even remotely possible? For lying and doing something my lawyers told me I could do? I have no baseline for any of what's happening.

Then, suddenly the prosecutors tell the judge I've indicated that I'm "willing to cooperate with the government in its ongoing investigation into Russian efforts to interfere in the 2016 presidential election."

I actually don't remember saying any of this to anyone—remember, I still don't truly grasp the deeper specifics of the case against me. Is it an open and shut case? Can I mount a strong defense? So why would I instantly cave? All I can think is that my counsel in Chicago discussed my cooperation. The Mueller team says they hope I will be a "proactive cooperator." In other words, a valuable informant.

I am baffled by this whole sequence of events. I've never been in trouble with the law. As I say, I've never had a speeding ticket. Exhausted, I'm taken to a new cell, where I meet my chicken wing-loving inmates.

The drug dealer asks me what I'm looking at in terms of a trial.

"I don't know," I say. "I've got no idea."

"They're just going to keep you here for a couple of months, probably," he says, sharing his jailhouse wisdom. "Unless you got somebody to post bail. But if you don't, then you might get a chance to go in front of the judge and appeal it."

It was shocking to hear this. He was talking to me as if I were a real criminal. Someone who is facing serious time. Someone who has no support network. Someone who was going to *really care* about the food menu. A prisoner. I am a prisoner. Jesus.

I don't say much. I'm just trying not to have a mental breakdown.

The next day, I'm released.

Just like that—no bail, no demands that I remain in custody, no nothing. After all this—sting operations, harassment, FISA warrants—they now know I'm in no way a Russian asset or colluder. They offer me a get out of jail free card. I am—in this moment—elated. Yes, I'm facing jail time, but for now, I'm sprung. All the anxiety about getting stuck in jail, waiting to make bail, and not being able to talk to Simona and my family and my lawyers just fades away. I am beyond relieved.

For a few seconds, anyway.

SOS SIMONA

As soon as I'm released and have a minute to myself—away from lawmen—I call Simona.

As I dial, I wonder what she'll think. Am I damaged goods? A crook? A criminal. The irony of all this is that I was just trying to be a team player with the Trump campaign and a good citizen who answered the FBI's questions without a lawyer present. And now I am facing felony charges.

The text I had sent her—the one at the airport saying I felt I was going to get stopped—was our last communication. I had left her in the lurch. She knew that the FBI had interviewed me because I mentioned it. But I didn't tell her I was a target of the investigation because, to be honest, I didn't believe I was a target. Anyway, she was worried. As she tells friends, she knew she had strong feelings for me, and she was concerned. After a day or two of wondering and waiting, she got an email from my first cousin, Tina, who she met in Greece.

"George has been arrested."

Simona has a torrent of questions: Why? What are the charges? How long is he in jail? How serious is it? But Tina only knows what she heard through the family grapevine, which isn't much. My arrest is top secret.

When we finally connect, I'm thrilled to hear her voice. It gives me hope that somehow everything is going to be alright.

It is also terrifying. How do you tell the woman you love that prosecutors are threatening you with twenty-five years in prison?

It's not great wooing material.

But Simona is outraged when I tell her the facts. She trusts me. She knows I'm not a crook or a spy. And she knows the character of people like Mifsud and Charles Tawil and the London Centre of International Law Practice. She's met these men. She's experienced it! She knows about the reputation of Link Campus Rome as a breeding ground for spies. The first thing she does is reach out to a high-powered attorney she worked with years ago as a trainee at top firm Mayer Brown—John Schmidt, who served as deputy counsel to George H. W. Bush in the White House.

It is so moving to me. I'm at the lowest point in my life, and even though she's 3000 miles away, she's doing anything she can to defend me by activating all her contacts to try to help me any possible way she can.

Eventually, she flies into Chicago. My life is pretty low key at this point. Nobody knows about my arrest or indictment. I'm not allowed to discuss it. I'm working with my lawyers.

One of the bargaining chips offered by the prosecution is that if I cooperate, they will drop the obstruction charge against me. At this time, I have no idea about the legal ramifications of my lawyers working out this particular deal. It is to be noted that by getting the obstruction charge removed, they are doing themselves a huge favor. By negotiating these terms and convincing me to agree to them, they eliminated any legal exposure for themselves.

CHICAGO BLUES

I arrive in Chicago and my prison-release euphoria has vanished. I feel like half a man. My life is in ruins. My passport has been confiscated. I have no ability to travel, which is what I do for work. So my business is shot. I'm facing huge, crushing legal bills. I'm in no shape to meet John Moody at Fox News, so I cancel that interview. I receive a secret, sealed indictment. It comes with a letter listing specific people I'm not allowed to talk to. This includes anyone involved directly or indirectly with Trump, as well as Joseph Mifsud, Olga (Putin's niece), and Sergei Millian. The strangest name of all is Oleg Lebedev. He lives in London, where he is married to my friend Maria Alexopolou. I guess he's a suspect because he's Russian-born. The FBI actually question me more about him more than about Mifsud.

Gradually I learn that my obstruction charge should never have been an issue. After I had met with the army of agents and prosecutors on February 16, 2017, I had asked my lawyers if I could deactivate my Facebook account, which is how Mifsud reached out to me.

Here is my own lawyer's submission to the court about this matter:

> Following the conclusion of his second interview, Mr. Papadopoulos asked his counsel whether he could deactivate his Facebook account so that certain individuals could not contact him in the future. Knowing that the deactivation of a Facebook account would result in the destruction of records relevant to the FBI's investigation, counsel advised Mr. Papadopoulos that he could deactivate the account.

I started thinking about getting new lawyers. But that was a daunting proposition. It would've meant delays. It would've meant paying more money.

Once I'm back in Chicago, my lawyers are nonchalant. They don't share my sense of outrage at all. I'm not even sure they believe or support me. The whole time, it's as if they know what the end of my story is going to be: cut a deal, be agreeable, plead out, don't upset the Feds.

Right away they tell me: Let's start talking to the prosecutors.

I'm naive, frightened George. I don't trust my instincts. I trust theirs. They urge cooperation. That will get me leniency, they say. The alternative—that we fight, that the FBI case is completely flimsy, that I never actually lied in bad faith—never comes up.

Under their spin, I decide that yes, I'll cooperate with the investigators. I meet to answer questions. Part of the deal, I'm told, is that I'm supposed to deliver the truth, the whole truth, and nothing but the truth. And that is exactly what I do.

But when I meet with the prosecutors, it feels like more of the same run-around that I went through with Heide, Mc-Swain, and FBI attorney Kevin Clinesmith. (By the way, Cline-smith, who led my second interview with the FBI, was fired by Mueller after he was found to rip into Trump in text messages saying, "Vive la Resistance!" His FBI pals, agent Peter Strzok and lawyer Lisa Page were also let go.) Maybe three percent of the questions are about Mifsud. I think it is bizarre. I keep thinking I can help my country by exposing this double agent. My mindset is, okay, I got in trouble, but at least they're going to arrest him, and maybe I'll be recognized for my service.

Dream on, George.

Meeting after meeting, hour after hour, the prosecutors did not care about this person who was really at the center of the scandal and intrigue.

It was entirely mystifying to me. They didn't want to know how he knew about the Clinton emails.

That leads me to wonder if maybe Joseph never actually knew what he was talking about. He certainly didn't share any reliable Russian sources with me. Maybe someone told him to say that.

To me.

And maybe the people who told him to say that were people investigating possible collusion between the Trump campaign and Russia.

Maybe these people were looking for a way to find evidence of collusion by planting a false flag story—that the Russians had dirt on Clinton—and then tracking the campaign to see who pursued the phony story.

That's the idea I started to think about. Not because I was

paranoid but because for six months, no investigator or pros-ecutor truly gave a damn about Mifsud.

What the prosecutors did give a damn about was finding out if I had shared Mifsud's information with anyone on the cam-paign. I got the sense that I was the lynchpin of their conspir-acy case, because if two or more people were discussing something like this, then the whole campaign was tarnished.

And so, possibly, were the election results.

In early August of 2017, I meet with prosecutors for the first time since my arrest. It's a hot, humid, Chicago summer day when just being outside can feel like torture. But arriving at the air-conditioned offices of the FBI's Windy City headquar-ters doesn't improve my mood. I walk through the metal de-tectors at the FBI's Chicago headquarters pissed off at the entire, absurd investigation. My attitude is that this is like a visit to a dentist—there's going to be discomfort and pain in-volved, but I have to do it to avoid even more pain.

My lawyers frame my position in a different way: I was just a little guy who meant nothing. "Just tell them what they want to hear"—this is how one of them puts it—"and we are done."

I am taken to the director of the FBI's massive office, which has a table that fits twenty-five people. There is an interactive, two-way TV. On the wall hang two pictures. Donald Trump and Jeff Sessions. "Am I here to testify against these guys?" I won-der. "Is that what they expect from me?"

That totally throws me for a moment. If they are not after me, who are they after? All I can think now is Trump and se-nior campaign members, one of whom—Sessions—indirectly runs the FBI!

But I've told these guys the truth from day one to the best of my ability. And I'm going to stay the course. I still feel loyal to the president, as he gave me a chance and even saved my job after the *Times* of London tried to make me look like a bully. But I'm not going to lie to protect Trump, and I'm not going to lie to get him, which is what I think these guys want. I am going to be completely truthful. End of story.

Assembled around me in the room are my lawyers, Mueller's prosecutors Andrew Goldstein and Aaron Zelinsky, FBI agents Curtis Heide and Michael McSwain, and a younger woman who seemed to be some sort of Russia specialist and behavioral analyst.

Goldstein kicks things off, distributing a slew of papers around the room, and immediately sets the tone:

"This is an agreement for a proffer," he says. "This is your last chance to cooperate, or we go to trial."

So the second sentence out of his mouth is a threat. The intimidation tactics that I felt during my airport arrest and subsequent arraignment are clearly in full effect.

Obviously, at this point, I want no part of a trial. I'm completely uninformed about the charges and the evidence against me—because I haven't seen the video of my interview or the accompanying transcript. All I know is what I've been told: I'm facing five years in prison for lies I don't remember making, and twenty years for obstruction because I followed my lawyers' advice and deleted my Facebook account.

The pressure from the prosecutors is relentless. Every time I open my mouth to ask a question or clarify something, Zelinsky says: "I am going to go home, and we will get ready for trial."

Eventually, the hardball attitude morphs slightly—and they start asking me questions. Actually, it's mostly one question, and it's the same question the FBI had asked me many times before: "Who did I tell on the campaign about the emails?"

At this time, I'm really nervous, because *I do not want to get a single fact out of place.* Lying—or the FBI's claim that I lied—is why I'm in this unfathomable situation. So I'm frightened. Every time I open my mouth, I could be setting myself up.

I try to dig deep into my memory, as I've done multiple times before. Other than telling the Greek foreign minister, I honestly do not remember mentioning the emails to a single person. Yet their very questions imply I did say something. It freaks me out.

"Calm down Mr. Papadopoulos, and tell us about your meeting with Sam Clovis after you met Trump," they say.

That is a "nice" question. Others are more specific and accusatory:

"You told Sam Clovis about the emails, right?"

"Look," I say, trying to defend my memory, my integrity, and myself. "I don't know if you are trying to implant a memory in my mind, or what. But I cannot sit here and tell you I told them about emails when I don't have a memory of doing that."

But this has no effect on them. We go back and forth about whether or not I had shared Mifsud's claim with campaign team members. For seven hours, in every possible manner, I am asked, "Did you tell him on this day?" or "Did you tell her?" They are relentless: Clovis, Lewandowski, Flynn, Manafort, Carter Page, person after person. There are moments when I feel dizzy, moments when I think about lying to get them off my back. But I don't do that. I tell them, "I don't understand. It's as if you're trying to implant a memory in my mind of something that never happened."

I remain utterly truthful. Seriously, I'm scared into blanket honesty at this point. I would have told them anything they wanted to know about me—my sex life, my finances, my most embarrassing teenage moment.

But the fact remains, I never told anyone on the campaign about Mifsud's tale.

Unfortunately, the truth was not what they wanted to hear.

No matter how much Robert Mueller and his team of FBI agents and prosecutors wished I had told campaign members about Mifsud's claim, I hadn't.

It. Did. Not. Happen.

The most bizarre meeting with prosecutors occurs shortly after Simona is interviewed by George Stephanopoulos in December of 2017. Simona did a fantastic job defending my work and reputation.

"George is very loyal to his country," Simona says. "He is already on the right side of history. I think he will make a big difference."

I love every second of her appearance—even when she jokes about me!

"I would love George to learn how to make a coffee because it's absolutely out of his skills," she tells the ABC anchor.

When the interview airs, the special counsel invites us to D.C. for the first time.

We arrive to find that the prosecutors are livid! They hated that someone was actually defending me and challenging their bullshit narrative.

"We will pull your plea agreement if she or you goes on TV again," Jeannie Rhee threatens.

I feel they are bluffing. It's hard to be certain, but I'm not convinced they have any truly compelling evidence against me.

The prosecutors ask to speak to my lawyers alone, and I sit in a room with Agent Heide. Just a few days earlier, a picture had been circulating on the internet—an image of Joseph Mifsud and UK foreign minister Boris Johnson. I ask Heide if he's seen the photo. Then I ask: "Why don't you guys arrest him? Haven't you told MI6?"

Heide gives me a blistering, stone cold snarl.

"He is a man of many connections," he says. "None of this would have happened if you just wore the wire."

At that moment, feeling his frustration and anger, I finally realize the FBI has set me up. Joseph Mifsud is no Russian agent! I've been duped into pleading guilty. What would have happened if I had worn a wire and met once again with the FBI? Maybe I could have asked him about the Russian email operation. But given the way the FBI has treated me, it's more likely Mifsud could have been instructed to spew lies about me. Lies that would be used against me. Maybe he would have gone on wild tangents—talking about how Trump knew everything and how I knew everything. If Mifsud was a plant for the FBI—and as I've said, the agents rarely asked me about him—or for a friendly Western intelligence agency, he could have been instructed to provide bogus or incriminating evidence that the agency could use to pressure senior members of the campaign or a policy advisor like me.

I stare back at Heide. There is no way I'm going to stop Simona from going on TV to defend me. She is a fantastic advocate. And these guys who are threatening me? They just want to use me for their war against Trump.

The investigators also ask me about a few Israelis I'd worked with in the past. They don't directly mention Charles Tawil, but when I say I met an ex-intelligence officer named Shai, Heide finishes my sentence, "You mean Shai Arbel?"—the man Tawil introduced me to. It was clear they knew about Charles, but they are less interested in him than they are in Mifsud. The same goes for Stefan Halper and Sergei Millian. They show zero interest in any of the people who have reached out to me to discuss Russia or intelligence or to offer me money.

As far as my Israeli connections go—and remember, Curtis Heide threatened to lock me up over them—I reiterate that I am in the energy business. I know these people because I'm respected in my field, not because I'm some sort of spy. I helped connect them with the Greek and Cypriot governments when no one else in Washington was interested.

They also want to know how I connected Trump to President Sisi of Egypt and ask about my connections to other foreign governments. At one point they threatened me with a Logan Act violation for helping Trump meet leaders!

Many of their questions feel hostile to me, as if they wanted to know my reasons and motives for helping connect Trump to other nations. Not Russia, but some of the countries I've mentioned in previous chapters: Japan, Taiwan, England, Greece, Cyprus, Israel, Egypt. These strike me as ridiculous questions. As a candidate, Trump has every right to develop international contacts, to forge relationships. And as a member of his policy advisory team, I have every responsibility to help him do that. I wasn't trying to stir up deals for the Trump business empire, which is something Michael Cohen has now admitted doing. I was committed to limiting radical Islam's sphere of influence in the Middle East and to curbing the anti-democratic empire of Turkey's strongman Erdoğan.

Yes, I wanted to build a career. Yes, I was excited by being close to power. Yes, I tried to excel at my job.

But I was trying to further America's interests, too. Always, always, always.

LUCKIEST MAN ALIVE

My time with Simona is fantastic and also agonizing.

My career is in shambles. My debt is climbing. We are staying at my mother's house while looking for a place to live. The best thing in my life is this passionate, beautiful woman who believes in me.

One day, while she's sleeping late, I can't take it anymore. I have to say what is on my mind. I tell her I know I don't have a job or any money. I tell her I'm going to get out of this legal mess. And I tell her I love her and I want to marry her.

"I don't have an engagement ring. All I have to offer is me. My devotion, admiration, and dedication. My love."

She says yes!

I'm sure it sounds strange to say, given my dire situation, but I feel like the luckiest man alive. When it comes to Simona, I still do.

Simona's relationship with me has costs for her. In October 2017, while I'm cooperating with Mueller's prosecutors, she gets a subpoena. She's told that if she agrees to cooperate, Mueller may rip up the court order. She weighs her odds. She calls the Italian embassy for advice, and they send her a list of $800-an-hour lawyers. She's worried because she's a foreigner. She wants to be able to get a visa to come and go as she pleases. I want that, too. In the end, she agrees to attend an interview with the FBI in Chicago—a much easier option than flying to Washington to testify in front of the Grand Jury.

"I'm a lawyer," she tells me. "I'll just do the interview. I have nothing to hide."

I'm nervous about this. I had nothing to hide and look what happened to me. "Simona," I say, "I don't know jack about the law. But I know this: If they ask you a question and you are not sure of the exact answer, make sure you tell them that. Tell them you don't remember. Or you can't be sure."

McSwain and a female agent interview her. They ask her question after question about me. They want to know if I had money and what she knows about my finances. They also ask about her own money. "They wanted to know how I can live this lifestyle," she tells me later. "I told them I am a professional lawyer. I have a successful career."

Then they tell Simona that I am in big trouble. They ask what she is doing with me. Was I worth the trouble?

Thanks, guys! Much appreciated. This is certified bullshit. Nothing was written in stone with Mueller's office regarding my future, but at that point, I wasn't actually in big trouble. I was cooperating fully. And things were in motion for a plea deal. I suppose pleading guilty to a felony in return for a reduced sentence is trouble—I don't wish it on anyone—but it wasn't the same kind of problem as facing twenty-five years in prison.

They also want to learn any and everything about Simona's ties to Russia, of which there were very few.

As I've written, so many people believe Simona is Russian or has close ties to Russia. Fortunately for these wrong-headed, clueless people, Simona has a good sense of humor. Plus, she understands the concern.

"I come from a political background myself," she says during an interview. "I used to work as a diplomat at the European Parliament for a few years, and this could be a red flag because many officials at the European Union actually use it as a cover-up for spy jobs."

As for the link between the two of us, she doesn't deny it's strange. "Of course this connection was highly suspicious," she tells the *Guardian* newspaper in a subsequent interview. After all, the man who told *me* about the Russian involvement is the same man who brought *her* to the London Centre—Mifsud.

But like I've told anyone who will listen, just because she's a worldly, gorgeous blonde who speaks five languages and has a mysterious, exotic accent doesn't mean she's a spy.

Ten days after her interview with FBI investigators, she leaves to close down things in London for good—her work, her apartment. When she gets to O'Hare Airport, McSwain is waiting for her at the gate! She is completely freaked out. "My eyes popped out of my head," she tells me. "I thought, 'Are they going to arrest me?'"

But she fares better than I do. They give her a secret phone number to call if she remembers anything or if anyone approaches her about Russia or collusion.

Or if she learns anything about her fiancé.

NEGOTIATION HARDBALL

The briefings continue with the prosecutors and my lawyers. I answer all their questions. Again and again and again. Now, as the prosecutors realize I have nothing to do with a campaign plot to collude with Russia, the finer details of the plea deal arise. What are they going to tell the judge, what kind of sentence are they going to ask for if I agree to plead guilty to a 1001 charge, the legal statute against lying to an FBI agent?

Well, they are out for blood. They want me to serve time in prison.

"This is bullshit!" I tell my lawyers. I am a pretty even-keeled guy, but this makes me livid. "I have done everything they've asked. I've spent tens of thousands of dollars defending myself while they searched for proof of a conspiracy that I knew

NOTHING about! They fucking tried to entrap me at least three times with Mifsud, Halper, and Tawil. And all they have are a few contradictions—as if I was trying to mislead them!"

I ask my lawyers if most people get prison sentences for 1001 charges.

It's unusual, they say. Very rare.

So why me?

They can't speak for the Special Counsel's Office, but the answer seems pretty clear. Mueller was appointed on May 17, 2017, to lead an investigation into "any links and/or coordination between the Russian government and individuals associated with the campaign of President Donald Trump." As far as I know, they've uncovered nothing. But they want to show that they mean business. Acting Attorney General Rod Rosenstein's appointment of Mueller gives the Special Counsel the power to investigate "any matters" that arise from his inquiries and to "prosecute federal crimes arising from the investigation of these matters."

I'm going from a so-called coffee boy for Trump to a de facto whipping boy for the Department of Justice. I may have absolutely nothing to do with illegal links or coordination with Trump or Russia, but I am going to pay anyway so that Robert Mueller and his henchmen—prosecutors Jeannie Rhee, Andrew Goldstein, and Aaron Zelinsky who write the plea offer to me—can show the world they've got muscle. They want to send a message: If anyone connected to Trump fucks with them—no matter how innocent they may be—they are going to jail.

My lawyers try to talk me down. They explain that although Mueller's team will ask the judge to sentence me to six months in prison, it is very rare that defendants facing a 1001 charge ever get jail time. If I am contrite and remorseful in the courtroom, my sentence should be minimal.

"Should be?" I ask. "Doesn't that mean the opposite can happen, and I'll get more time?"

Yes, they say. But it's improbable.

On October 5, 2017—nine months after Curtis Heide and Michael McSwain convince me to answer questions without a lawyer present—I receive an official letter detailing a plea agreement.

It calls for me to plead guilty to the 1001 charge of lying to a federal agent.

It specifies that the SCO will request I receive the six-month prison sentence.

It also calls for me to waive any right to appeal or challenge the sentencing I will receive—which seems like a denial of my fundamental due process rights. I was under the impression that the right to an appeal—or apply to appeal—was a fundamental. But apparently it's not—if the Special Counsel is trying to make an example out of you.

I must also agree not to seek any restitution for costs I've incurred from this misguided investigation.

I'm not happy about all this. It seems like a crappy deal. If somehow the judge is hostile to me, I might get saddled with spending five years in prison and paying a $250,000 fine—the maximum penalties. That is a worst-case scenario, of course, but it's worth considering.

Then there is an even more frightening scenario.

I get word that if I don't okay this plea agreement, the Special Counsel will file much harsher charges. All their questions about my contacts with Israel appear designed to provide them with ammunition for another, far more outrageous charge—

that I was operating as an unregistered foreign agent for Israel, and they will hit me with FARA charges.

This is as chilling as it is false. I was never an Israeli agent. Never. But FARA charges are a whole other life-ruining ballgame. I'm not a lawyer, but from where I sit, it's a fine line from being a foreign agent to being a spy. I don't know how serious the SCO is about ginning up such bogus crimes against me. But after everything that has happened, I don't want to find out. Andrew Goldstein looks at me across the table and says, "Robert Mueller is a war hero. No amount of political pressure you might have will stop this from getting to you."

That is a strange remark. I wonder if they are worried about my political contacts abroad ruffling feathers.

"It is in your interest to plead guilty."

My experience with the justice system has been sorely lacking when it comes to seeing justice prevail. I discuss things with Simona. And I say, okay. I don't want to admit any wrongdoing—I mean, what have I done? Failed to accurately remember the sequence of events during two of the busiest months of my life? I never denied meeting Mifsud. I volunteered his comments about Russia having Clinton's emails. So what were the "lies"?

I'm thoroughly pissed off about all this. But I want to put it behind me. I want to marry Simona and get on with living. I agree to say I'm a criminal, even if it's not true.

"Okay," I tell my lawyers. "Let's get it done."

CHAPTER 13

THE GRINDING
WHEELS OF JUSTICE

I T TAKES ELEVEN months to get from the plea deal to the actual "end" of the case—I put those quotations marks there because in some ways it hasn't ended. During that time, while Mueller probes the real criminal activity of former Trump campaign chair Paul Manafort and former Trump personal lawyer Michael Cohen, I become a media punching bag as news filters out about my arrest. The plea deal is filed on October 5, 2017, but it doesn't get unsealed until October 30—the same day Paul Manafort and Rick Gates are indicted.

Manafort and Gates are hit with multiple charges—from "conspiracy against the United States" to "conspiracy to launder money" to "unregistered agent of a foreign principal"—many of which are much more severe than the charge against me. But headlines and TV talking heads still treat my plea as big news because I'm the first person from the Trump campaign to be charged with wrong-doing that is vaguely connected with the collusion aspect of the case. Mueller actually charged someone before me, a Dutch lawyer named Alex van der Zwaan who worked for Manafort and his partner Rick Gates. (According to sentencing judge Amy Berman, Zwaan was "caught red-handed" lying to investigators and was even found to have communicated with Gates and a person with Russian intelligence ties.) Although he is married to the daughter of Russian oligarch German Khan, the guy has zero direct links to the Trump campaign, unlike me.

So my arrest story generates far more ink—almost all of it negative. This makes perfect sense in the sensationalist, headline-driven world we live in. I am a "former Trump advisor," and that makes the charges against me—lying to the FBI during their investigation—important. I'm proof, in the eyes of so many Trump haters, of the president's shady dealings and desire to collude with Russia to win the election.

I hate seeing my name used in this regard. The fact is, I was forced to agree to this deal, forced to accept that I lied. But as I say, I didn't make false statements to protect the president or hinder investigators. Without consulting my calendar or my emails, I did not accurately remember the timeline of events. I think most reasonable people would agree there is a difference between being wrong—getting mixed up on facts—and lying. If lying is in the eye of the beholder, and Mueller—who has spent millions of dollars investigating Trump and collusion charges—is the beholder, then it stands to reason his team is going to say I'm guilty of lying. The Mueller Investigation needs convictions, not just for public relations purposes but as a scare tactic for future suspects and people of interest. I'm also perceived as guilty by the partisan, Trump-hating press and for never-Trump true believers who think the FBI can do no wrong or doesn't have an agenda. For them, I don't deserve any benefit of the doubt.

The hits start coming.

To Trump loyalists and Trump himself, I'm a pariah and nobody. The day the agreement is unsealed, White House press secretary Sarah Sanders tries to put as much distance as she can between the campaign and me, telling reporters my role "was extremely limited; it was a volunteer position. And again, no activity was ever done in an official capacity on behalf of the campaign in that regard." You know who else were "volunteers?" Jared Kushner, Paul Manafort, and Steve Bannon. So Sanders, who I didn't work with, is either uninformed about my role—and doesn't know about the various meetings and interviews I conducted at the direction of the campaign—or she is lying.

Trump himself piles on: "Few people knew the young, low-level volunteer named George, who has already proven to be a liar."

I'm reasonably sure Trump has no idea at the time that I helped arrange for him to meet Egyptian leader Sisi or paved the way for his meeting with Abe or defended him to the British press. I believe someone educates him on my role and what I've endured because less than a month later, on November 18, 2018, he unleashes a tweet about the FBI that sounds a lot like what I've experienced: "They are screaming and shouting at people, horribly threatening them to come up with the answers they want."

One day after my plea is unsealed, on October 31, Michael Caputo, a communications adviser to the Trump campaign who worked for Russian interests repeatedly, including a stint at Gazprom-Media to improve the image of Vladimir Putin in the United States, goes on CNN. "He was the coffee boy," Caputo says. "You might have called him a foreign policy analyst, but if he was going to wear a wire, all we would have known now is whether he prefers a caramel macchiato over a regular American coffee in conversations with his barista."

Caputo's remarks are nasty and mean-spirited, which makes them newsworthy when they should be laughable. I can't speak to his role on the campaign because we barely interacted. So I have no idea what his opinion is based on. Perhaps I shouldn't have been surprised. When Corey Lewandowski was replaced by Paul Manafort as campaign chairman on June 20, 2016, Caputo tweeted, "Ding dong the witch is dead!" This was at 8:49 in the morning; that evening, having embarrassed the campaign, he resigned.

I guess CNN is happy to air guests who talk or tweet before they think.

The most frustrating thing about my arrest and plea deal being made public is that I still can't say anything. I can't defend myself or explain the nuances of what happened. Listening to all this is tough. I read the headlines and see my reputation destroyed on a national stage—and I can't defend myself. I am itching to get out there and tell my side of things, but I have to wait until I am sentenced before I utter a word in public, or risk incurring the wrath of the special prosecutor and the judge presiding over my case. Meanwhile, why is my right to a fair and speedy trial dragging on for months and months? The prosecution keeps asking for extensions, so they don't expose other aspects of their investigation. Even though I want to put this behind me and eliminate the lawyer fees that every delay costs me, I agree to the postponements. It's the right thing to do.

Fortunately, Simona has no restrictions on what she can or can't say. She starts giving interviews to the media. She appears on Sean Hannity's Fox News show. She tweets. She starts making inquiries about finding me a pro bono lawyer to consider legal alternatives for me. The closer we get to the actual sentencing, the more strident and furious she becomes.

In defending me, Simona now becomes part of the collusion story. She's been a person of interest to Mueller's investigation team, and now she's of interest to the media. And you can see why. She looks and sounds like a femme fatale double agent in a James Bond movie. Blonde, sexy, with an exotic accent.

The fact that she knew Mifsud for years and worked for him just before we met seems completely suspicious on the surface. The fact that she sounds, to some people, like she's Russian or Slavic only adds to the mystery about her. The anti-Trump forces love this. To them, she's further proof that the campaign was corrupt and so am I.

STORMY WEATHER

The 2017–2018 winter is rough. I'm not working. My mother gives Simona the cold shoulder. So does my father. It doesn't make for a warm family vibe in Chicago. And the fact that I'm not making any money doesn't make things any easier.

Simona has something to tell me. She is pregnant! We are thrilled. The timing isn't perfect, obviously, but this is excellent news. I can't lie, it's also utterly daunting, given so much uncertainty in our lives.

We want to get married—to show the world we are united. That we are not spies, and that we fell in love despite so much madness. Ideally, we want to get married in Italy. But I can't travel due to my legal nightmares, and it is likely I won't be able to travel for a year after my sentence—assuming the judge doesn't hit me with a considerable sentence—so exchanging vows overseas isn't an option. We move out of my mother's house into a small studio apartment. Simona has some savings, but not much. I have to borrow money to live and to pay my lawyers.

Then Simona loses the baby. We are heartbroken. We spend our time huddling and healing. After months in the frigid Chicago cold, we decide to move to California in the spring. The world seems even colder when on February 2, 2018, Congressman Devin Nunes releases a memo stating that in July 2016, FBI agent Peter Strzok opened the investigation into Trump-Russia collusion based on "information" about me and not on the Steele Dossier. It's hard to fathom that I was Suspect Zero. Or make that target zero. It seems like decades have passed since Christian Cantor urgently introduced me to his "girlfriend" Erika Thompson, who then urgently arranged for me to meet Alexander Downer.

That set the whole thing in motion.

And rocked the Trump presidency and ruined my career.

WE DO!

In early March, we make another decision. Us against the world!

We get our marriage license. Should we do it? Should we wait? Finally, we set a date, Thursday, March 2, 2017. The night before the big day, Rhonda Schwartz and Brian Ross come to Chicago to interview us. We all go out to dinner. I like Rhonda and Brian. They are good, hard-working reporters. I know they have befriended us because we are part of the biggest political scandal in years. But I also think they have been fair when it comes to reporting my story. They understand that I've been unfairly targeted. During dinner, away from their cameras and microphones, they ask about our future. Simona tells them we are going to get married the very next day.

"Oh my God!" Rhonda says, "Congratulations. Is it a private ceremony?"

"Right now it's just the two of us."

"We've got to be there! Can we come?"

They join us the next day in the basement of Chicago's City Hall, where civil weddings have taken place for over a century. It is nice to appear before a judge without worrying about FBI charges. Simona looks breathtaking in an elegant, sleeveless, cream dress. As Cook County traffic court Judge Marina Ammendola leads the brief service, I feel completely at ease and in love with my passionate ally and paramour.

As Simona herself says, our relationship is filled with coincidences and contradictions. She's Italian; I'm from a pretty typical Greek-American family. She's a lawyer who loves fashion, movies, and acting; I'm an energy policy guy who loves to go clubbing and solve geopolitical problems. She worked for the Socialist Party in Europe; I'm a conservative. I'm quiet and calm; she's fiery and animated. And strangest of all, we met because of a man named Mifsud, who sold both of us a total bill of goods.

After exchanging I do's and one of the best kisses in my life (our first kiss was pretty good, too), we go to Taxim, a Greek restaurant in Wicker Park, to celebrate.

One last note about our wedding witnesses: The Trump-Russia scandal ended up hurting Rhonda and Brian's careers, too. Just eight weeks earlier, on December 1, 2017, Brian reported that a source told him that Michael Flynn was set to testify that during the campaign Trump instructed him to establish contact with Russia. Rattled by the report, the stock market dropped over three hundred points. By the evening, Brian corrected his report: Trump was the president-elect when he requested making contact. But Brian was suspended for four weeks by ABC News, and the newshounds eventually ended their work with the network.

THE SENTENCING ORDEAL

On August 17, 2018, Mueller files a sentencing memorandum, basically outlining the government's version of the case. It recommends the judge sentence me to between one and six months in prison and accuses me of hurting the collusion investigation. I've already talked about my "lies"—but here is the Special Counsel's Office stretching the truth in its way:

"The defendant's crime was serious and caused damage to the government's investigation into Russian interference in the 2016 presidential election," Mueller writes. "The defendant lied in order to conceal his contacts with Russians and Russian intermediaries during the campaign and made his false statements to investigators on January 27, 2017, early in the investigation, when key investigative decisions, including who to interview and when, were being made...the defendant repeatedly lied throughout the interview in order to conceal the timing and significance of information the defendant had received regarding the Russians possessing 'dirt' on Hillary Clinton, as well as his own outreach to Russia on behalf of the campaign. The defendant's false statements were intended to harm the investigation, and did so."

This is slanted and biased reasoning. I never intended to harm the investigation, and I seriously doubt anything I said marred it at all. I initially played down Mifsud's importance not to protect the Trump campaign, or "harm" the investigation, but to protect my own ego. Was that a mistake? Maybe, but that is the truth! Mifsud was an embarrassment to me. Everything he told me turned out to be smoke and mirrors. The man fabricated Putin's niece for me, and I fell for it! Can you imagine how stupid I felt about the whole thing? I wasn't trying to shield the campaign, either. That's because Mifsud never really touched the campaign, except via my emails—which relayed his B.S. I felt foolish about that, too. In my first interview, I didn't think, at first blush, the FBI should waste its time with a total clown. Of course, when I thought about the gravity of Mifsud's remark and brought it up to investigators, they didn't seem interested! I also want to point out how devious the wording of the memorandum is. Some of the SCO's most damning statements imply a connection between my "lies" and the hindering of the investigation. But there is no actual correlation. Here:

"He made his false statements to investigators on January 27, 2017, early in the investigation, when key investigative decisions, including who to interview and when, were being made."

This is meant to suggest my statements derailed the FBI. But it conflates two things—my answers and their decisions—without actually saying how my supposed lies impacted their decisions. There's no actual proof anything I said "harmed" the investigation. To suggest that I damaged the inquiry is even more absurd when you consider that they already had the answers. They knew all this—they knew I had talked to Mifsud—and I admitted to this in the first interview. They knew I had spoken to Downer. They claimed to know everything about me and Israel. So what did my botched timeline mean to them? It means they now had the legal framework to charge me with a crime! Before I talked to them, I had done nothing wrong. After I talked to them, they could put me in jail.

There have been reports that my comments contributed to the FBI failing to capture Mifsud while he was in the United States. But this, too, is entirely wrong—unless the FBI is capable of time travel. Here's an email from Mifsud trying to connect with me.

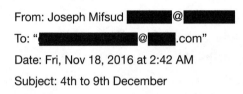

From: Joseph Mifsud ███████@█████████
To: "████████████████@███████.com"
Date: Fri, Nov 18, 2016 at 2:42 AM
Subject: 4th to 9th December

Dear George,

I hope you are well. As mentioned I am going to be in the US during the dates above. Where and at when can we meet? I would be willing to travel to where is more convenient for you. There are a number of issues that I would like to discuss with you.

Kind wishes, and best regards,
Joseph

Note the dates. Unless Mifsud changed his ticket, he was long gone from the United States when the FBI came to talk to me. There was nothing I could have contributed to their efforts in catching this jerk unless I agreed to Heide's request to wear a wire—a request that, curiously, doesn't appear in any of the Mueller court documents. That interview seems never to have happened.

MY DAY IN COURT

My sentencing hearing is Friday, September 7, 2018. I appear before US District Judge Randolph Moss at the E. Barrett Prettyman Courthouse in Washington, D.C. My lawyer Tom Breen is there as the lead attorney who will present my case to Judge Moss. Meanwhile, the three people who love me and support me most in the world—Simona, my mother, and my father—are in the courtroom, putting up a brave front. I am beyond grateful they are here.

Andrew Goldstein, a big, broad-shouldered attorney, formerly of New York's Southern District Court, is the point man for the Special Counsel's Office. With him are Aaron Zelinsky, also from the SCO, and my old pal, Special Agent Curtis Heide from the Federal Bureau of Investigation.

I've never been at a sentencing trial, so it is all new to me. The judge seems like a straight shooter. He lays out the steps of the hearing and who he wants to hear from to determine the sentencing. He notices that the obstruction charge against me has been dropped and says it will not influence his decision. But he also wants to hear about it. He says the Probation Office has recommended I be sentenced to "a sentence of 30 days imprisonment, 12 months of supervised release, no fine, community service, and a special assessment of $100."

He invites Goldstein to address the sentencing issues.

He launches into my so-called damaging lies. Here's the play-by-play:

Mr. Goldstein: The defendant could have corrected the record at any time before then [July 27]. The investigation had become highly public; he knew it hadn't gone away. But he chose to leave his lies standing as they were.

It was not until he was arrested that he—

Judge Moss: So can I ask you about that? He was interviewed and made the false statements in January of 2016 (sic).

Mr. Goldstein: That's correct, Your Honor.

Judge Moss: He then came back in with counsel in February—

Mr. Goldstein: In mid-February, that's correct.

Judge Moss: In mid-February. Was there any attempt or effort at that point in time to correct the record?

Mr. Goldstein: Not by the defendant, no.

Judge Moss: Okay. And did he repeat any of the lies or was the topic at the interview just different topics?

Mr. Goldstein: It was largely different topics.

Judge Moss: I see.

Mr. Goldstein: But at that point, he had counsel and there was no effort in that interview to correct any of the misstatements or the lies that were told in the first interview.

What Goldstein fails to note is that I NEVER SAW a transcript of my first interview. So how can I correct something if I don't have a record of my supposed misstatements? And how can my lawyers advise me to correct those issues? Goldstein makes it seem like I was ducking and lying when it was to the investigators' advantage to leave my "lies" in place—so they would have a bargaining chip over me. Before my February appearance, I had gone over the timeline. I had refreshed my memory. So I would have been happy to set the record straight. But we didn't have a copy of the record!

The judge points out to Goldstein that the majority of cases involving lying to the FBI end with probation sentences. "I believe that over the past ten years, there have been seven cases in this district in which there was a violation of section 1001," he says. "And I believe of those seven cases, that [the van der Zwaan Case] is the only one where there was a term of imprisonment. Now, obviously, I don't know exactly what happened in all of those cases. Nationally, I believe that in just shy of sixty percent of the cases, the sentence is one of probation."

I love hearing this. It makes me think the judge is a reasonable man. But it's tough, because Goldstein keeps pushing for me to wind up behind bars. He tells the judge that in my case, lies were "allowed to persist for many, many months in an investigation of clear national import where the defendant knows and understands the importance of the investigation" which is different from previous cases.

When my lawyer Breen begins to talk, he fails to note that specific lies were not pointed out to us, which would lead to a delay in correcting the record. He also falls on his sword—or rather impales me—by agreeing that I did a stupid thing by lying to the FBI. I hate hearing this. But this is what I have to admit—even if it's not entirely accurate. Breen does a pretty good job, though, of noting that it was a bewildering process, that I spoke without a lawyer or notes present—which suggests my truth issues may have been more innocent than the FBI is trying to make out.

He also does a good job of summarizing my mindset and my focus on connecting Russia to the campaign, and how the Mifsud email statement wasn't that interesting to me because I was focused on arranging a meeting between the campaign and Russians. But his closing argument sells me down the river—along with Trump.

"On January 20th, the president of the United States, the commander in chief, he told the world that this was fake news and a witch-hunt," Breen says. "Seven days later [Papadopoulos] is brought in for the interview."

According to Breen, this event influenced my answers.

"The guy he worked for, who he wanted to see president of the United States, is telling everybody that the investigation these fellas talked to him about is fake. And that's the mindset going in there."

Then he adds that my motives "for lying to the FBI had to do with loyalty to a candidate and loyalty and concern for his future with the Trump administration. That's what it was."

This is only half true: I was concerned about my future with the administration. Loyalty to Trump, however, was never the issue—I wasn't trying to protect him from anything because, as far as I was involved, there was nothing to protect Trump from. The campaign was interested in improving relations with Russia, which was never a crime. I didn't see how my actions had anything to do with the Special Counsel investigation.

For better and for worse, the momentum of a prosecution's case can dictate a defense's response. I imagine few defendants are 100% satisfied with the statements and admissions that must be made to obtain a deal. It is a give-and-take situation. Even my own statement causes me problems because my lies, such as they were, were never malicious.

Here's what I tell the court:

Your Honor, in January 2017, I made a terrible mistake for which I have paid dearly, and I am terribly ashamed.

My parents, who are in this courtroom today, raised me with the principles of honesty and respect for the law. When I lied to the FBI, I cast aside those principles and compromised the person who I am. Please understand that when I told those lies, my life was in a whirlwind. I had just left a presidential inauguration and all the festivities that were involved with it. I was surrounded by important people and the promise of brilliant opportunities. I was young and ambitious and wanted to serve my country at the highest levels. I was excited to be part of something that I sincerely believed in.

When the FBI came to my home, I knew that there was an incipient investigation into Russian efforts to interfere in the 2016 presidential election. I wanted to do my best to help this investigation while simultaneously creating distance between the issue, myself, and the next president of the United States. I understand now that in trying to do this, I was not honest and I might have hindered the investigation.

My interrogation covered a myriad of topics regarding my interactions with Sergei Millian; whether Israeli officials were cultivating me as a spy; the dossier; my knowledge of any potential campaign collusion; and of course the now infamous Professor Joseph Mifsud.

While I told the FBI that Joseph Mifsud informed me that the Russians have thousands of Hillary Clinton's emails, I hid many aspects of my relationship with Joseph Mifsud. That was wrong, it was a crime. I consider myself a patriotic American who in no way would ever hurt his country. Serving in the United States with pride is all I ever wanted to do.

In hindsight, lying to federal agents about such a critical issue could have harmed our nation, and for that I am deeply embarrassed and personally ashamed.

Since my name was released publicly, my entire life has been turned upside down. Friends stopped returning my phone calls. People point and snicker, and I have been terribly depressed. I am most saddened by the stress of my actions and the public shaming have visited on my loving family and my wife. It will take me a lifetime to repay them for their support.

While many may think that I deserve it, I hope that I do not deserve it. I hope to have a second chance to redeem myself. I made a dreadful mistake, but I'm a good man who is eager for redemption. I also hope that me standing here in front of the Court and you, Your Honor, and the public today signals to all future and current witnesses in this investigation that this investigation has global implications and that the truth matters.

I'm grateful for the opportunity I was given to assist in this investigation. I was young and naive, but I've done my best to atone for my mistakes. I have nothing but respect for the Court and the legal process, and I am ready to accept my sentence. Thank you, Your Honor.

After my apology to the court, Judge Moss takes a ten-minute break to gather his thoughts. I gather mine. Ninety-nine percent of my statement is true. The one percent that isn't is, unfortunately, the most damaging part—where I admit to lying and damaging the investigation. I had to use those words and own them because those were the charges the prosecutors insisted on hitting me with. I was faced with a choice: accept the charges that I lied or face FARA charges. I made a deal. A deal forced on me.

As for "lying," I am truly sorry I didn't get the dates right when I talked to the FBI agents. Still, I was never told what my false claims were. At the official "second" FBI meeting—run by a lawyer so virulently anti-Trump that Mueller dismissed him—I was never asked about my previous responses, so how could I amend them? To me, that's as much the investigators' fault as mine.

Now I smile at Simona, and I wonder if my words resonated with the court.

Judge Moss returns. He speaks about how sentencing is the hardest part of his job, and that he recognizes that even a short sentence is of enormous importance to a defendant. Then he weighs in on the nuances of the case, saying: "I don't have any reason to believe and I don't think there's any reason in the record to conclude that Mr. Papadopoulos had any desire to aid Russia in any way, to do anything that was contrary to the national interest."

My heart swells at that. It is true.

Then he gets down to business:

"I'm going to impose a sentence of 14 days of incarceration, 12 months of supervised release, 200 hours of community service, and a fine of $9,500."

He also says that my apology rang true to him. He was initially going to sentence me to thirty days in prison but says, "The reason that I came down from that to the fourteen days was by what I perceived to be Mr. Papadopoulos's genuine remorse about what he did."

On one level, Judge Moss's sentence and his words are a true gift. A minimal sentence that says: George Papadopoulos had nothing to do with collusion with Russia; he's guilty of one thing: poor judgment.

Who among us isn't guilty of that?

The difference is that most people's bad decisions don't land them in the middle of a multimillion-dollar federal investigation. I just got lucky.

Thinking about the judge's strong pronouncement absolving me of collusion, I begin to hope that the political establishment will allow me to have a second act.

That allowance has started to happen in some quarters. Key figures have come to my support, including Fox's Tucker Carlson and Sean Hannity on the right and figures like Tom Arnold on the left. Their support and the support of so many other Americans who read deeper into the investigation mean the world to Simona and me.

That said, there are moments in the case I wish I could do over.

When Judge Moss asked me if I was "fully satisfied with the representation of your counsel in this case?" I answered yes.

Since meeting with my new lawyers, New York-based criminal defense experts, I regretted pleading guilty. We surrendered rather than calling the SCO's bluff. There was never any pretrial discovery. We never saw—or at least I hadn't seen—the transcript of my interview, so all we had was the prosecution's word regarding what I had said. And we caved.

As for my admitting to a crime—I'm upset about that, too. I guess I've made that pretty clear. Do I think I lied and hindered the investigation? No, not intentionally! I answered questions without checking my email, without looking at my calendar. Of course, I'm going to get things wrong.

I'm sure some people will think these are sour grapes on my part. After all, the short sentence sent a huge message to the world: my crime, such as it was, was minimal. I wasn't a treasonous, treacherous, Russia-loving dirtbag. Unfortunately, for those who never read below the headlines, I've been tarred as some kind of Moscow cheerleader, or under-handed campaign operative with a Russian wife who is a spy. I'm a convict—the first member of Trump's campaign team to go to jail. These are things that can't be undone. They make it that much harder for me to move on. I can't reach the doubters, the haters, who know nothing of my story—a story that is completely unbelievable unless you can look at it from the beginning and see the obvious threads and connections and omissions.

The world knows George Papadopoulos pled guilty. Few have any idea about the other players who were operating backstage: Alexander Downer, Sergei Millian, Stefan Halper, and, of course, Joseph Mifsud. These are central figures who worked to put me in a bind. How are they related? Who was pulling their strings and why?

It's time to find out.

CHAPTER 14

CONNECTING
THE PIECES

A S I SAID in the opening of this book, I was the right guy to be the wrong man.

I was idealistic, trusting, and naive, and that made me a perfect fall guy—just the kind of mark to be portrayed as a bad actor in a manufactured Russia-collusion narrative.

How did I get caught up in the biggest scandal to rock American politics since Watergate? The short answer is this: It was about killing three birds with one stone.

By targeting me, the deep state of former Obama and Clinton-loving lawmen aimed to:

1. Protect the outdated US-Turkey power structure—and the billions of dollars of arms and energy deals at stake—by removing me from Trump's team.
2. Cripple the Trump campaign and administration in order to prevent any warming of relations between the United States and Russia, even though both countries face huge threats from radical Islam and China.

3. Send a message to the rest of Trump's team—thus sowing chaos and distrust inside and outside of the administration.

Before Russia-Gate broke, I was not widely known to the media, but I was well-known to policymakers and special interest groups who believed the US relationship with Turkey was sacrosanct.

To these people, I was an advocate of potentially dangerous ideas—isolating Turkey, creating an alliance with Israel, Cyprus, Egypt, and Greece—that threatened to upend the status quo in the Mediterranean. This realignment concept was frightening to ideologies at the State Department, the CIA, the NSA, as well as many major foreign powers, including England, Australia, and players in the multibillion-dollar energy and arms sectors.

When the *Washington Post* revealed I was on the Trump advisory team, people familiar with my work became alarmed. For those with a vested interest in protecting Turkey's authority and the West's relationship with that country, my proximity to Trump was a threat. In 2015, former ambassador Matthew Bryza made it very clear to me that the State Department didn't appreciate my meddling and neither did he. Now, I was working with a presidential candidate who had pronounced me "an excellent guy" in the *Washington Post*.

That announcement and my presence at the March 31, 2016 advisory meeting at the Trump Hotel in Washington, D.C. set everything in motion to make me a target, putting me in the collective sights of the FBI, CIA, MI6, Mossad, and Turkish and Australian intelligence. There's been a lot of talk about having me testify on Capitol Hill. If the democratic chair of the House Intelligence Committee wants to get to the bottom of how an innocent patriot working for the Trump campaign was targeted, I would fully support him!

Here is what needs to be investigated:

a) Did Turkish intelligence, hostile to my ideas, contact American deep state operatives?
b) Did nervous policy wonks in the State Department write memos to the FBI and CIA about my working with the Trump campaign?
c) Did one of the cold warriors attending the Trump advisory meeting—freaked out by my meet-with-Russia proposal—betray the campaign by sounding an alarm to intelligence operatives?

My reputation as a political heretic made me a person of interest to intelligence services around the world. I advocated a few radical ideas to strengthen America's geopolitical standing, and I had access to a presidential candidate. And then—BANG!—there are all these meetings I have over a three-week period: Mifsud, Christian Cantor of the Israeli embassy, Erika Thompson of the Australian High Commission, Alexander Downer, two US embassy spooks, and British members of parliament. Everyone was vetting me. Everyone was talking to me about Trump. And almost everyone asked me about Russia.

Mifsud, who set everything in motion, remains the man with the most mysterious motives. Who did he work for? Why was he approaching me? Who directed him to set me up and why? He has gone underground. In fact, when investigators lost track of him, there was even a rumor he was dead. But he's very much alive and hiding under a new identity, according to his personal lawyer Stephan Roh.

Alive or dead, let's dig a little deeper into Mifsud and who he was working for.

When Nagi Idris of the London Centre of International Law Practice heard I was working for Trump, he immediately said I had to meet someone who would help me. He then called in our colleague, Arvinder Sambei, a woman who had previously represented FBI interests in London. She was delegated to arrange my meeting with Mifsud.

Speaking of meeting with Mifsud, investigative reporter John Solomon wrote an article for *The Hill* revealing that the FBI interviewed Mifsud in February 2017 about our meetings and also sent an email summarizing the interview. Mifsud reportedly denied telling me about the Clinton emails. But that didn't create any delay in the investigation. They were interviewing him the same time as they were quizzing me!

It is also curious that Mifsud worked at the Link Campus Rome, the school with deep connections to Western intelligence agencies. Mifsud has a Swiss-German lawyer named Stephan Roh, who is a part owner of Link Campus and regards Mifsud as a close friend. Roh has been very clear about Mifsud's allegiances to Western intelligence. Mifsud "had only one master: the Western Political, Diplomatic, and Intelligence World, his only home, of which he is still deeply dependent," Roh has written in a self-published book about Russia-Gate.

Was Mifsud working for those intelligence agencies when he fed me the line about Russia and Clinton's emails? I believe so. Here's why: Mifsud had barely any Russian contacts that I could see. He was an abject failure in this regard, introducing me to a woman he falsely and bizarrely claimed was Putin's niece—a relative, by the way, for which there is no real-world corollary (the Russian leader doesn't, in fact, have a niece)—

and, via email, Ivan Timofeev. I'm not sure he knew any other Russians. So it seems very likely someone with a very specific purpose in mind armed Mifsud with the Russia-and-Clinton email ammunition.

And if he *did* have useful information about Clinton's emails, he *still* could have been working for Western intelligence. As the Steele Dossier shows, there are clearly people who work both sides of the Russia intelligence relationship. Insiders become sources, double agents, or informants, in a sense.

What was the point of Mifsud telling me about the Russian hack? He never said, "Let your people know." He never offered to share the emails with me. He never told me what shocking or embarrassing things the emails revealed. In all our exchanges, he never followed up on the remark, and I didn't pursue it at all. My sole goal, as I've said until I'm hoarse, was to arrange a meeting.

So why? Why did he tell me? More and more I come back to my original connection to Mifsud. A former FBI employee contacted him and put us in touch. Then Mifsud, a Western intelligence operative, tells me about a Russian plot. Then, one day after Trump's first foreign policy speech, Obama-loving Israeli diplomat Christian Cantor helps engineer a meeting with Australian High Commissioner Alexander Downer, a man who works with current and former intelligence operatives on a daily basis and sits on the board of one of the largest private intelligence firms in the world. Are you with me?

I don't remember saying anything to Downer about Russia or Hillary Clinton. But as I've said, the High Commissioner seemed to be taping some of our conversations, and I suppose he may have baited me into saying something about the election. But what if my memory is correct, and I didn't say anything? What if Downer had been told by the FBI or MI6 that another asset—Mifsud—had mentioned the scammed email and Russian interference to me. What if Downer got a request to file a report—a bogus report—alleging I had said something about Russia and Hillary Clinton. This is not far-fetched. Remember: Downer has admitted I never mentioned emails or hacking. It's safe to assume his cable, which officially set off the investigation, was a pretty weak, bare-bones document. According to him, I said something about the Russians having a surprise.

It wasn't much, but it was all the FBI needed. It gave them an excuse to start digging into Trump's campaign.

One last thing about Downer. The day my name surfaced as the subject of an investigation, he posted a picture of himself with the Turkish ambassador in London. He has since taken down the photo. Was that coincidence or was he trolling me? Draw your own conclusions.

So that is how my nightmare—and a deep state conspiracy—began. Someone—we may never know who until FISA warrants are declassified—raised a flag and said, get this guy Papadopoulos away from the candidate. If Trump wins, he could ruin our relations with Turkey. Plus, he's talking about working with Russia. I believe at some point the CIA or FBI said, let's make it a two-for-one deal and taint him with the Trump-Russia-collusion angle, and get rid of him. And boom! Downer sent his alarmist cable—about something I don't think I ever said—and gave the FBI the excuse it needed to start an investigation.

But the FBI wasn't done. Now, having fed me a line about a Russian plot, they needed to see how this shocking story would spread and who would do the spreading. I'm sure they hoped I was involved in the dissemination because they didn't have any hard evidence against me. Downer, it seems, didn't have me on tape—or if he did, what he had wasn't incriminating or admissible. And so, I was pursued by a number of operatives.

First, the two intelligence guys from the US embassy wined and dined me and got nothing—because there was nothing to get. In July 2016, Sergei Millian came calling. I now think of Sergei as the businessman equivalent of Mifsud the professor. An operator, a networker. A guy who sells whatever he's hired to sell and tells whatever he's hired to tell. One month before he contacted me, Source D—as Millian is called in the Steele Dossier—was also photographed at a business conference in St. Petersburg with Oleg Deripaska, the Russian billionaire and close associate of Vladimir Putin who employed Paul Manafort. Was he conspiring with Putin's people? Millian is an American citizen, so if that were the case, I think he would have been arrested a long time ago. Instead, he seems to have vanished from the entire Trump-Russia story. To me, this suggests he was a deep state informant working to foment a Russia-collusion storyline by talking to one of Steele's sources. It is interesting that the wildest, kinkiest story in the entire Steele report comes from a guy who lives in the United States. That makes the dossier seem like a flimsy tabloid report. Just because someone says something doesn't make it true.

The fact that Millian has disappeared from public view and his name has all but disappeared from the Special Counsel Office's investigations provides further proof he was a Western intelligence asset. I believe Millian was on the FBI payroll. And I believe Mifsud was either a CIA or MI6 operative, but it wouldn't surprise me in the least if another foreign power—Italy? Turkey?—had him on their payroll.

Millian, of course, struck out with me. I was gun shy about Russia. And my campaign contacts—I can't speak for others on the team—had cooled to the subject. When I think about

Millian's outrageous business proposals, funded as they were by mysterious Russians, I realize by agreeing to them, I might have been in violation of the Foreign Agents Registration Act—the same disclosure requirement that Michael Flynn and Paul Manafort ignored and were nailed for. Although FARA has been widely ignored for years in Washington, the Special Counsel's Office has dusted the statute off as a prime weapon to get members of the Trump circle to talk. It seems, in retrospect, that Millian's offer—to set up a Russian-funded consultancy— might have been a setup for me to give the FBI another reason to arrest me.

When Millian's early overtures failed to generate a gotcha moment, the deep state decided to order out for help. Enter Stefan Halper, ex-CIA employee. There is little question Halper was being used by intelligence in a sting operation against me. Since our meeting, he has been identified publicly as an FBI informant. Who else, besides me, was he trying to inform on? Carter Page for one. But he even met with Sam Clovis, who headed Trump's foreign policy team. I also think there is a possible connection between Downer and Halper. I believe Downer's evidence against me—an alleged single remark about Russia and Clinton—was weak and that Halper was, ideally, going to be the source who would nail me. If Halper had done so, investigators wouldn't have had to expose Downer's involvement, which is really beyond anything a High Commissioner should be directly involved in. Both Downer and Halper have connections to Hakluyt, the private intelligence agency. They are both pals with Richard Dearlove, the former director of MI6. Finally, Halper's whole line of questioning and innuendo mirrored the attack-style and subject matter of Downer. The Walrus—that's how I think of him—

steered our conversations from Turkey to Russia. He gave it his all to get me to talk about Russia and collusion. Note to his handlers: he gets points for trying but none for style. He was rude, insulting, and boorish.

Soon after Halper whiffed, as I understand it, the FBI got a FISA warrant on me (they may have had one far earlier; I have no idea). The investigation then dragged on for months and all the FBI had on me, apparently, was my faulty timeline regarding my conversations with Mifsud and an obstruction charge that wouldn't stand up in court. Those were not very glamorous charges. The FBI needed to do better! So what do they do? They find a trusty old informant with more connections than O'Hare Airport: Charles Tawil.

Tawil had a great cover story: as a wealthy, super-connected businessman. He had zero information on his LinkedIn page because he didn't need LinkedIn. He's old school, and he dropped Mossad references, talking about his corrupt president pals in South Africa and Uganda. He was the kind of guy who stepped out of the pages of a John le Carré novel—as generous as he was devious. He played his role hard. He flew to Mykonos, and he offered to fly me and Simona to Israel. When I showed up, he gave me $10,000 in cash.

Tawil has given interviews denying any links to intelligence operatives. He also charges that I asked him for cash and that I sent him an email after our misguided and murky trip to Cyprus. I'm not surprised by his denials. But his track record speaks for itself: bragging about his friendships with despots and criminals, his shadowy existence as a businessman, his constant referrals to intelligence agencies, and the WikiLeaks revelation that he was a U.S. State Department informant. As for that email, I did send it. I was still trying to justify or resolve the $10,000 that my lawyer held in Greece, so I kept in touch and even tried introducing him to potential partners. I'm still waiting for him to pick up his money.

What were Tawil's true motives for the payment? People in the business world generally don't go around handing out thousands of dollars without agreements in place. The $10,000 cash payment was, in theory, a perfect setup. I have to give all the parties involved credit—FBI, CIA, Mossad, whomever, take a bow! It was a great plan. And if it had worked, well, TRUMP RUSSIA-GATE ADVISOR NABBED WITH THOUAND AT AIRPORT! is a much, much better headline than TRUMP AD-VISOR LIED TO FBI! Luckily, I sensed something was truly wrong. I gave the money to a lawyer in Greece.

After fourteen months of being spoon-fed conspiracy infor-mation, questioned by bullies, lured by honeypots, taped and monitored by the FBI, and handed $10,000 in cold, hard cash, the only thing I did wrong was misstate a timeline of events to two federal agents.

My story is part of a larger story. The story of Trump and the story of stopping Trump, or trying to. The Trump presidency was the primary target of all this insanity.

It's a story of abuse of power and prosecutorial overreach. That said, what I'm going to say here may upset people on both sides of the political spectrum, but I have to say it, so brace yourselves.

The movement to investigate Trump for collusion connec-tions is, on a certain level, completely understandable. There is now significant evidence that Trump did have business con-nections with Russia both before and during his campaign. The fact that he blatantly and repeatedly denied these things means he was, theoretically, in a position to be blackmailed and exposed as a liar.

By Russia.

First and foremost, I am a patriot. I don't want our president to use political power to endanger American interests for personal profit. I hope one hundred percent of Americans agree with me. But I also don't believe law enforcement agencies should enlist informants to create evidence of wrongdoing where none existed beforehand.

Listen, I'm just collateral damage. I'm a guy who got caught in a counterintelligence storm called Crossfire Hurricane. It was a sinister battle, but it wasn't about me at all. Whoever got Mifsud to tell me about a Russian plot was planting evidence to hurt Donald Trump's chances of winning the Republican nomination and of defeating the presumptive Democrat nominee Hillary Clinton. That evidence was used to further a diabolical and terrifying storyline: That Russia was interfering in a US election to promote its agenda. And it may be true. Parts of the Steele Dossier have been confirmed. Suspected Steele sources in Russia have been found dead under suspicious circumstances. A number of Russian operatives have been convicted of meddling in the election. But at least one part of the Trump campaign—the part I was involved in—showed no interest in collusion. Period.

Other relevant details need to be stated when evaluating the Trump-Russia investigation.

It is a fact that when the investigation started, Barack Obama, a Democrat, was in the White House. All senior branches of law enforcement answered to him. It is a fact that FBI chief James Comey, a Republican, owed his job to Obama, as did Comey's predecessor—a guy name Robert Mueller. Another virulent Trump critic, Obama appointee John Brennan, was running the CIA when the investigation opened. It is also a fact that Obama had every reason to detest Trump on an entirely personal level. For years Trump led the insulting, demeaning, and thoroughly debunked claim that Obama was born in Kenya and therefore was an illegitimate candidate. Lastly, it is a fact Obama's former secretary of state was Hillary Clinton, Trump's main adversary in the 2016 election.

Entire books have been written about Hillary Clinton's alleged abuses of power. I don't want to get into them here. But I do want to say that all these facts point to an understandable anti-Trump and anti-Republican bias at the highest levels of the Obama administration. I don't believe President Obama issued a covert "get Trump" order. But I do think there was a climate of distrust and suspicion surrounding the candidate. Out of that distrust, deep state plans were hatched to investigate the candidate.

Our intelligence operatives did what they do: They gathered information. They assessed it. They reported their conclusions to the chain of command. Intelligence assessments are not an exact science. And in concocting an investigation, gung-ho prosecutors and agents unfurled a wide net. A vast net, as we are seeing. Unfortunately—for me, for the nation, for Trump—they got tangled in it.

By floating a conspiracy—having Mifsud tell me about Russia—intelligence agents created a self-fulfilling prophecy. Intelligence agents launched an operation that doubled back on itself each time they sent in more clowns—Downer, Millian, Halper, Tawil—to try to prove collusion against me. Instead of achieving success—as they have with Manafort, Flynn, and Cohen—they just added to the noise, having more reports leaked out, rumors swirled of nefarious doings, and so the specter of conspiracy spread without proving a damn thing. Now, we have half the world believing I'm some pro-Russian devil and that my wife is, too. And that Trump needed Russia's help to beat the most divisive candidate in America: Hillary Clinton.

And that's ironic and unfortunate because I wasn't conspiring with *anyone*. And Robert Mueller's minions, in their feverish aim to get the goods on Trump, conspired with informants to create and catch criminals. But they didn't need to do that, either, because there seem to have been a number of bad actors in Trump's orbit who left paper trails behind. Unfortunately, there seem to be just as many bad actors in Mueller's world. I genuinely hope they clean up their act. I'm not holding my breath.

CHAPTER 15

INCARCERATION & INSPIRATION

I N THE DAYS after my sentencing, I grew more and more incensed over the prosecutorial abuse I'd just experienced.

Simona, an experienced lawyer, was equally outraged, if not more so. She had to cope with the wreckage caused by the FBI and Robert Mueller's over-zealous targeting—the crippling legal bills, a reputation in ruins that makes it hard for me to find work, my battles to fight off depression.

And she had been baited and abused, too. The press speculated on her motives—implying that her connection to Mifsud was proof she's a spy. People on social media constantly malign her and accuse her of being Russian. It made us both crazy.

So we started to defend ourselves and reclaim our reputation by telling the truth everywhere and anywhere. Fox News's Sean Hannity and Tucker Carlson had us on their shows and helped get our side of the story out. They understood that we were victims of the war on Trump and Robert Mueller's scorched earth investigative tactics.

The more I talked about this nightmare journey—not just

in public, but with other lawyers—the more I regretted my guilty plea. I had been targeted, set up, and then given questionable legal advice. I began to discuss withdrawing my plea. I hired new lawyers, and we searched for ways to avoid or push off my prison sentence. We even began drafting a request for a presidential pardon.

But here's the thing I learned about most presidential pardons: Historically the people who get them have some kind of political capital to trade on. They have connections with people in power, they have money that makes them influential donors, or they have some kind of social movement or organization advocating for them, which can translate into influencing voting blocks. Me? I had very little political capital. And Trump, fighting a public relations war with the Special Counsel, didn't seem likely to inflame things by issuing an immediate pardon to a Mueller target.

While exploring the pardon route, Simona and I moved to Los Angeles so she could pursue her career and I could look for new business opportunities. As the date for my incarceration grew closer, it became clear my options were limited. My scant resources were no match for the Special Counsel's Office. So much for truth and justice.

SET UP TO BE SENT UP

Finally, the clock ran out. I was going to serve jail time and pay my "debt" to society.

Simona and I were bottoming out. I had $100 in my bank account. Simona had gutted her savings. I wasn't even sure how I was going to get to Wisconsin and turn myself in. Greyhound bus? Hitchhike? Jump a train? Money, legal woes, worrying about Simona—I was on a razor's edge, stressed out, racked with insomnia. Pissed at Mueller. Pissed at the FBI. Pissed at myself for being ambitious, patriotic, and naive. If I'd just gone to law school, none of this would have happened.

Out of the blue, a film producer named Stephanie Fredricks reached out to us. She'd been following my story. She'd seen Simona on TV giving interviews. She had a proposal—to film a documentary series about our story and our struggle to clear our reputations, fight back against the abuse of justice perpetuated against us, forge new careers, and repair our relationships with our family. A reality show, sure, but one that put our battles front and center.

I listened to her proposal. It was manna from heaven. Not only in terms of providing us with a much-needed financial boost but one that would help me tell my story, clear my name, and publicize the deep state war that is being fought in this country.

Stephanie wanted to start immediately. Simona and I looked at each other. We had the same reaction: Absolutely! Our lives had been exposed on a daily basis. Newspapers, TV news, and magazines had made a fortune splashing—and battering our names—on shows and websites. Why shouldn't we have a vehicle to counter all that B.S. and show the world what had happened to us, who we had become, and what we hoped to achieve.

ROLL 'EM

We started filming four days before we got to Wisconsin. The cameras were set up around our small apartment to capture our daily lives—from the moment we woke up to when we finally turned off the lights. They sure picked a stressful week to start filming. Prison loomed. I had been told I was going to a low-security facility. There would be a lot of white-collar criminals doing time for financial crimes, people with drug records, stuff like that. But all I knew about prison was what I'd seen in the movies—gang violence, prison rapes, segregation, abusive jailers. On top of everything, it was going to be freezing cold, with crappy weather. I wasn't sure I would last a day. And worst of all, this made my plea agreement totally real. I would serve time even though I'd done nothing wrong.

I'm a positive person, so positive and trusting that I've ended up screwing myself by associating with the likes of Joseph Mifsud, Sergei Millian, and Charles Tawil. I tried to maintain this perspective, but flying into Chicago, I just sank deeper and deeper into a black hole. The day we drove to prison, Simona started talking to me about my lawyers and how they wanted to discuss alternative strategies. I just snapped. I was furious at the world. At everyone. The cameras were rolling, and I turned to Simona: "I don't want you to come with me!"

She was shocked. It was totally unfair and self-centered of me. She'd been with me every step of the way. But it was humiliating going to prison. I didn't want her to see it. I didn't want the world to see it. But now, it was going to be on TV. Simona shouted back at me. She got in the car. We were both fuming, sitting as far away from each other as possible. I was just stewing, feeling sorry for myself and mad at myself for acting like a jerk. As we got closer to the prison, a cell phone rang. A pastor from Texas wanted to talk to us.

"Brother George, Sister Simona," he said. "I want to pray for you."

He told us that we needed to remember that the light comes after the darkest hour. He read us a Psalm, and it was impossible not to be moved. Simona felt the same way. I pulled her close—the partner I would not be able to hold again for two weeks. I felt my eyes tearing and shut them. All the tension and anxiety that had us screaming at one another evaporated. I felt nothing but love and gratitude for Simona—and regret that I was leaving her.

DOING TIME

We arrived at Oxford Federal Correctional Institution. The main building was a low-slung, red brick one. FCI-Oxford is a medium security prison with a connected minimum security camp, which is where I was assigned.

From the street level it looked about as ominous as a town library or post office. As our driver is parking the car, a woman runs out of the office yelling, "NO CAMERAS!"

"Everything is going to be fine," I say, trying to sound sure of myself as I hug Simona one last time.

I ran in. A bunch of camera crews and photographers were running around trying to get a shot of me entering prison. Inside, I was greeted by a pleasant, courteous woman. She welcomed me and told me, "I'm not speaking for the Bureau of Prisons, but as a private citizen, I want to say that I think what happened to you was terrible."

Then she started telling me that from the administrative perspective, my sentence was more trouble for the prison than for me. "We just want the situation to be as pleasant as possible and that no one bothers you. If you need any help, please contact us."

I was very surprised by this. Then I realized: I'm in Trump Country—I'm going to be okay.

The prison guards who checked me in were very friendly. I stripped out of my suit and tie so they could see I wasn't smuggling any contraband. Then I changed into my prison jumpsuit. One of the guards said he thought my sentence was "bullshit."

"Yeah," I said, "I am a casualty in the war against the president."

"Listen, you don't have to worry in here," he said. "This is Camp Cupcake."

"You're not with any cho-mos, either. So you don't have to worry about that."

"What's a cho-mo?"

"Child molester."

My prison education was underway.

In my new prison duds and all checked in, I walked into an open space where I was going to meet one of my cellmates. There were a bunch of people around watching TV, reading, and talking. Somebody let out a whoop, people were looking in my direction. The guys started clapping—the prisoners and the guards—and rising to their feet.

They gave me a standing ovation.

I was totally stunned. My reaction at first was to smile and laugh. All these inmates and all the guards knew who I was, and they appreciated what I'd been through. They knew I'd gotten a raw deal. It was really cool and totally unexpected. It was like my own *Cool Hand Luke* or *The Longest Yard* moment. And it was really comforting. I'm going to be okay here, I thought.

After that I was introduced to my new "cellie"—that's what prisoners called their cellmates at this place. His name was Frankie, and he was an elderly white guy with white hair and blue eyes. He took me to our cell, which had two bunk beds divided by a desk and window. My other cellmates were David Staral Jr., the former owner of the Chicago Rush arena football team, who was doing time for defrauding investors, and a guy named Gino who was in on a drug charge.

The camp reminded me a bit of a college. There's a library with hundreds of books and copies of the *New York Times, Wall Street Journal,* and *Chicago Sun-Times* lying around for anyone to read. There was a gym that looked better than the one I paid a membership for out in the real world. This one had a full basketball court. There was a chapel. There was also a clean cafeteria serving mostly edible food.

My stay was hassle free. The most awkward moment was when inmates approached me to ask if I could help them. Guys came up and started telling me how they'd been rail-roaded and received bullshit sentences. Then they'd ask if I could help them get lawyers or funds. I guess they thought that since I was on TV that meant I had clout. I would tell them, "Look, man, I totally believe you. But I'm struggling to get by and develop a support network myself."

One of the most interesting things I discovered was that there's a class system inside the prison. One of my cellies paid another inmate to clean, cook, and do odd jobs. I walked into my cell and my bed was being made for me. While that sounds bizarre, people need money in prison. There are prison jobs, but the pay is beyond slave wages. And while some people have resources and get funds from outside to spend at the commis-sary, others don't. And so they earn cash from more well-heeled inmates.

I walked into the prison chapel and did a complete double take. There was an older man who looked exactly like my grandfather back in Thessaloniki. His name was Marvin Ber-kowitz. He was seventy-one years old and serving a twenty-year sentence on embezzlement charges. I spent most of my days talking to Marvin. He was a fascinating guy. As you might expect for someone who apparently swindled more than a million dollars, he had the gift of gab. But I got the sense he really could walk the talk. We talked about an enormous range of subjects, from Bible stories to Plato's *Republic*, to how to start a corporation to the vast subject of taxes. Listening to Marvin, I couldn't help thinking, "Why is this guy here? He's so damn smart, how could he wind up in prison?" The short answer, I guess, is he got caught. But in his case, I'd say it was a combination of greed and being too smart for his own good.

The most difficult moments of my stay involved Simona. The first night there I was walking toward my cell when one of the inmates, Tim Roth, calls out, "Hey, look at the TV." Simona's face filled the screen. My wife! On Tucker Carlson. I was so proud of her, and yet it was difficult to watch. Listening to her, seeing her defending me was great. But the facts she laid out also made me angry. I was a bundle of emotions.

Simona came to visit me toward the end of my sentence, and that was also challenging. Everything about the visits was awkward: We couldn't touch or hold each other. I sat in one plastic chair, and she sat in another. Ever the fashionista, she told me I looked cute in my prison duds. But the cold, public setting really threw me. It was the opposite of intimate, of private, of free. I didn't want either of us to be where we were, and so I was lousy company. Simona told friends I was sad. But I was actually okay in prison. Just seeing her made things hit home.

I ended up serving twelve days, getting two days off for good behavior. And when it was time to leave, my mood immediately shifted. I was feeling great. My mindset was much stronger. I felt, in a way, rejuvenated. I had more energy and more hope—which is something I'd had a shortage of for the last year. I felt like new challenges and adventures awaited me. While I was in prison, I thought about my next moves. I had a book to finish. I had a TV show to shoot. I thought about politics. The midterms had just happened, and a Republican congressman had been bounced out of Reagan Country. I thought, maybe I should consider a run. I decided to give it serious consideration. Who better than to try to check the deep state than a guy who's been a victim of it? Who better to discuss prison reform than someone who's served time (although I admit, it wasn't that much time)?

Simona came to pick me up on December 7, and we hopped on a plane to get to Washington, D.C., where I was scheduled to speak the next day at the three-day American Priority Conference.

TRUMPING DISASTER

As we flew, I tried to think about where I now stood on the political spectrum and how I might summarize the events that had led me to the conference.

I continue to support Donald Trump. He's said some good things about me and some demeaning things. And sure, some of his people called me a "coffee boy," but I've been called worse—far worse by an army of conspiracy theorists and Trump haters, who continue to assault and blame me on social media every single day. While Trump has not been everything I'd hoped, he has been under assault, too. Some of this is his own doing—certain senior members of his team should have been vetted more carefully.

Trump has had forces both inside and outside the government—deep state operatives and foreign intelligence organizations—conspiring to taint his campaign and his presidency. Government figures in London ranted about him to me. So did Australians. I'm sure the Germans and French, the leaders of the European Union, were terrified by him. Israeli officials, members of a country that is perhaps America's greatest ally, even seemed baffled and worried by him.

MI6 operatives—probably coordinating with the FBI—conspired to send agents to bait me in the hope that I would taint the rest of the campaign with collusion fever. Only God, James Comey, Robert Mueller, and perhaps FISA court judges know what other operations they ran at other members of the Trump team. I have no doubt the Australian, Israeli, Turkish, and other operatives were involved as well.

AMERICAN PRIORITY

I was nervous as I arrived at the conference. I was now, officially, an ex-convict. I thought the crowd would be supportive, given other speakers at the event included right-wing controversy magnets Mike Cernovich and Laura Loomer. But I was now, officially, a law-breaker, and I was worried.

I shouldn't have been.

As I walked into the conference hall at the Marriott Wardman Park with Simona, the packed crowd erupted, giving us a standing ovation. Strangers were patting me on the back, and I actually saw a few women with tears streaming down their cheeks. It was an incredibly gratifying and moving moment. These were people who supported me, who came from all over America to hear me speak out about how and why I became a target.

Simona and I spoke on stage for about an hour with right-wing blogger Mike Cernovich. It was very cathartic for me to share everything that happened—to go on the offensive and fight back after spending so much time being badgered and threatened and bullied. The session flew by, and I exposed what I called "the corrupt foundation of my case": that Joseph Mifsud—who, according to his own lawyer, was an operative for Western intelligence—was used to lure me and others into colluding with Russia, something I would never dream of doing. When I got off stage, I was engulfed by a throng of well-wishers who wanted to shake my hand, pose for a picture, and share words of support. The organizers came up to me and thanked me. They wanted to focus on the future: "We think you have a great future in politics. We want to be your base and help you." We talked about creating a movement. It was exhilarating.

I didn't feel like an ex-con. I felt like a patriot and warrior. And that is precisely what I plan on being.

ACKNOWLEDGMENTS

I'd like to acknowledge Dan Bongino, who kept my story alive for months and months, and congressmen Mark Meadows and John Ratcliff, who allowed me the opportunity to testify on Capitol Hill. And thank you to Tom Flannery and AGI Vigliano, plus the team at Diversion Books for helping make this book a reality.

Finally, I'd like to thank my mother, Kiki Papadopolous.

INDEX

Index

Index

Index

Index

Index

Index

ABOUT THE AUTHOR

George Papadopoulos became the first person to plead guilty in connection with the Mueller Investigation when—on October 5, 2017—he conceded that he had lied to the FBI about a conversation with a professor during which he was told that Moscow had "dirt" on Hillary Clinton and "thousands of emails," according to court records. Papadopoulos is a former advisor to President Trump and Secretary of Housing and Urban Development Ben Carson. A University College London graduate, past Hudson Institute analyst, and career oil, gas, and policy consultant, he was sentenced to fourteen days in jail, fined $9,500, and ordered to complete two hundred hours of community service and one year of probation after he served his sentence. A native of Chicago, he is married to Simona Mangiante and now lives in Los Angeles.